Final Act

Cliff Myers
Final Act

ISBN 979-8-90001-804-1

Spines

Final Act

Share The Journey As An Old Entrepreneur Creates His Final Business - Cherry Blossom Creamery

Cliff Myers

Contents

Journey with an old entrepreneur while he builds his final business

The story of Cherry Blossom Creamery

By Cliff Myers

Preface

For many of us, retirement is not the glimmering destination that it is often portrayed. I would be more than capable, particularly if my good health continued, to fill my days with activity. Playing tennis four or five times a week, making sure I got my ten thousand steps the other days, would and will continue to satisfy my need for exercise. Preparing meals from scratch, taking part in my grandkids and daughter's lives, and maintaining several rental properties will fill a portion of a week. For eight months of the year, working in my gardens adds exercise and a chance to connect to the soil. Sporadically planning and executing stain glass projects releases some of my creative impulses.

Then there is always the idea of travel. Much as I want to see and experience new things, I am at heart a homebody. I love my small house with its beautiful screened porch. I love that it is decorated with my wife's beautiful artwork and that there are even a few pieces of my stain glass work as well. It is a house that Sue and I have lived in for over forty years. It is a house where we raised our kids. It is a house that has been home and a final resting place to numerous dogs, several cats, a few hamsters, and one chameleon. It is a house that we very slowly remodeled in many stages for it to become the house we wanted, even though we had always cherished the little Cape Cod from the moment we had purchased it. So, ten days into a vacation, I am ready to return to Hershey, the only place I have lived aside from my time at college.

I am in no way unappreciative of the great life that I enjoy, but at seventy years of age, I still felt at loose ends. I have worked almost every day of my life since the age of fourteen. In the beginning, for others, including the Hershey Orchards, Hershey Park, Hershey Bakery, the Hershey environmental labs and then finally at the Hershey Country Club as the tennis director. I also worked in enterprises that I had created, including a sporting goods company and a concrete garden statuary company. My latest enterprise was a landscape company that, after seventeen years, I had just sold to a couple of its employees, and now I am all but removed from that, my latest company.

I need to begin something new. A new challenge, facing a new set of problems to solve, and a chance to create a company that could be managed in a different manner from my previous attempts. What could be big enough to engage my interest and yet modest enough to allow me, with a more limited time horizon, to build a successful business? More importantly, what would be the metrics that would be used to define its success? Realizing that in all likelihood this would be the final chapter in my story, I needed to be certain that I was not repeating myself. Using my past entrepreneurial experience, I had some guidelines for any new venture. I wanted a business that was in control of the product it sold. I did not want to be so dependent on suppliers for my inventory as I had been in the sporting goods business. I wanted the flexibility to create new items without the costs and time requirements that my statuary business required. Producing artwork of which molds could be made required long lead times and considerable expense. I had despaired of solving the labor issues that the very seasonal landscape business presented. My new business had to offer the opportunity for year-round and fixed hours for its employees. Most of all, I wanted to create a product or service that would set itself apart from its competition.

As a lifetime small business owner, I had the opportunity to share my concerns and listen to the concerns of many other small business owners. To someone who is not a small business owner, you would expect the largest problem that a small business faces is competing with other businesses or with much larger enterprises for customers. Surprisingly, that is seldom a major concern. If we offer appropriately priced, quality goods or services, there appear to be enough opportunities for all of us.

What is the big worry? There are two questions that often seem unsolvable: How to scale your business? How to add another location, or a second truck or another crew that no longer is under your direct supervision and yet retain the profitability and quality that you had before this expansion? There is the related concern, which is how to have a successful and quality-driven business that allows you to have less day-to-day operational personal involvement. In any of my ventures, I had not solved these two related questions. I am not alone. Most of my entrepreneurial friends continued to successfully operate businesses, but only by spending an enormous amount of their time running those businesses.

Could I use fifty years of experience to answer these questions? If, from the onset of a new enterprise, everything was viewed as having to eventually stand by itself without my direct supervision, could the business become scalable or at least able to operate by itself? This would require written policies and procedures beyond anything I had attempted in the past. Along with this detail would require proper and extensive training and promotion of staff. Hopefully, a new business would afford me an opportunity to grapple with old questions in a new way. I think I was ready for that challenge.

In this COVID time, I had grown so weary of how business was being conducted. It was almost universal. Either you encountered massive incompetence, blatant inattentiveness, or plain unfriendliness. Many times, you would find all three. When your experience was not marred by any of these, you were so surprised that you probably shared that unusually great experience with many of your friends. Would it be possible to create a business that was a refuge from the rest of the retail experience? Could I create a place where customers were greeted in a friendly manner? This would be a place where orders were filled quickly and accurately. It would be a place where employees knew their products, and where those products were so outstanding that your customers would say Wow. This would be a place with a clear mission, and the employees felt connected to that mission. Could I create a business that if I had shopped in that business, I would return to again and again?

Could batch-created ice cream be the vehicle to manifest this vision? Homemade ice cream, manufactured and served in a beautiful setting with indoor and outdoor seating, would be the reason for customers to congregate. A location that provided plenty of parking and ease of access would be necessary to achieve the no-hassle refuge state that I was envisioning. Other details sprang to mind. As thoughts tumbled through my mind, the large multi-panel stain glass mosaic that I had begun took on new significance. The subject was a cherry tree in blossom. The name for the ice cream store became apparent. It would be named

Cherry Blossom Creamery. If this massive, creative endeavor of a cherry tree-based mosaic could be completed, it would be installed across from the ice cream store.

Now all that I needed to do was find the right location. I needed to learn how to make ice cream. I had to obtain the proper permits for whatever location I decided upon. I needed the proper permits for the manufacturing and sale of ice cream. If I were going to begin this venture with the idea that it would be able to stand on its own, I needed to generate the process and procedures to allow the business to do just that. I no longer worried if there was enough to engage me in this process; instead, I was overwhelmed.

CHAPTER 1

WHERE TO BEGIN?

As a preliminary step, I reached out to a company, Commercial Refrigeration, that I had used for HVAC work at one of my commercial properties. I had noticed that they posted on their trucks that they provided refrigeration services for restaurants. I made a quick phone call to Tim, whom I had worked with in the past, and explained that I was thinking of making my own ice cream. His ready and enthusiastic acceptance of this idea initially surprised me, but then I realized that he was going to be able to sell me a lot of equipment if I were to move forward. He assured me that he and his company would be able to help me obtain all the refrigeration equipment that I would require.

For the specific ice cream equipment that I would need, he referred me to another local company, Love's Thermal Systems, located in nearby Wilkes-Barre. He had the owner and president, Rich Love, contact me. In a matter of a few days, I was driving to

Rich's office to have him demonstrate the equipment that I would need. After that visit, Tim and Rich formulated a list of both the equipment I would need to produce my ice cream and also the equipment I might need to sell that ice cream.

As impulsive as this might appear, I had not gone into this ice cream business totally blind. Before I had contacted either Tim or Rich, I had spent some time on the internet searching for courses on how to make ice cream. I had found a site called Ice Cream University. The site was a creation of Malcolm Stogo. His biography was quite impressive. He had even been inducted into the ice cream hall of fame. Who even knew that such an organization existed? Malcolm offered a combination of online and hands-on seminars. He also offered several books that he had authored.

If there was one method of learning that I was comfortable with, it was studying books. My order for "How to Succeed in the Incredible Ice Cream Business" and "Incredible Ice Cream, Making it your way with passion" arrived at my house. I quickly devoured the books. Aside from increasing my excitement for my new venture, the books offered a guide as to the equipment that I would need for my store. I was able to fine-tune the list that Tim and Rich provided, and before long, we had specifications and prices for the essential equipment.

There was a lot of equipment that I would need. If I wanted to maximize the store's success, both Malcolm in his books and Rich in his phone calls insisted that I needed to offer soft ice cream as well. To do that, I would need a soft serve ice cream machine. To produce and sell the handmade ice cream, I needed a hardening cabinet, a large reach-in refrigerator, a storage freezer, dipping cabinets, a display freezer, a three-compartment sink, a separate hand sink, and a worktop refrigeration unit. It was

January of 2021, and I had a list and prices for what I needed. More importantly, I had Tim and Rich and Malcolm, even if it was remotely, to help guide me.

Most new business owners know what it is they want to produce or what services they wish to provide. For me, I want to produce great ice cream. I want it to be the freshest, tastiest, creamiest ice cream that people have sampled. I want amazing flavors. Along with traditional dairy-based ice cream, I want to offer lactose-free alternatives. I want this alternative ice cream to be so good that it is barely distinguishable from our regular ice cream.

That was the easy part. Now the bumpy journey begins. How do I learn to make ice cream? Once it is produced, how do I sell it? Am I going to attempt to develop wholesale accounts or find a location to sell it by the scoop? Or both? Where am I going to produce my superior ice cream? Where is the location where I am going to sell this great product? Who do I purchase the equipment from to manufacture and then dispense my ice cream? What equipment do I need? What permits do I need from the state? How do I even answer so many of the questions on the application when they refer to specific information that I will only know once I have the location? Will the location that I choose be properly zoned? Will I be allowed to produce my ice cream there? I will need to obtain a building permit. I will need a sign permit. I will need an architect to stamp the application for the building permit. Is there adequate parking? Once the number of allowed parking spaces is sorted out, how much indoor and outdoor seating will this allow?

Then to more pleasant questions. What else should be offered aside from ice cream? Crepes? Bakery items? Snacks? Coffee station? Simple hot items? If I can clarify what else I want to offer, I will need to find either sources for them or the proper equipment to make them myself. What is my concept for how the store, if it is to be a scoop shop, should be painted? What can I use to cause kids to want to return? A model train? An aquarium?

What seemed at first blush to be a simple idea that would allow me to produce ice cream has quickly morphed into a nightmare. My longtime friend, my own anxiety, is with me more and more. I need to give myself a pep talk. I need to remind myself that I have considerable business experience. I have started several businesses. I have had employees work with me since I was twenty-five. Maybe having all of this past experience is what is responsible for how discouraged I am when I look at all that needs to be done.

I am sure that it was less stressful to begin a business before I had all of this experience. The great business consultant, Michael Gerber, has a saying: "beginner's mind, blank sheet of paper." If you don't know how difficult something is, you often overcome obstacles that have defeated many others. I need to channel that beginner's mind. I need to separate the questions I have and work on them one at a time. More importantly, I need to have the faith that as I begin to bring this concept to fruition, I will find the answers that I need. If I occasionally fail to do something properly, I can ask forgiveness and stumble forward.

For months, I have struggled with what will be my initial concept. Of course, I am going to make batch-style ice cream. I can envision my customers being wowed by my innovative flavors and their great taste. After either finishing their cones or discarding their empty dishes, I can see them stopping by the display freezer and taking a long time to decide just what wonderful flavors they will take home to enjoy later.

Then more questions arise. Do I offer milkshakes? Do I create different sundaes? Are there food items that should be on the menu? Do I need a coffee service? How about a soda dispenser? I love crepes, and there is only one other place in Hershey that is currently making crepes. Should I combine crepes and ice cream? It sounds great to me.

I have reluctantly added soft ice cream as I have been advised by everyone that I have spoken with in the ice cream business that, since kids prefer soft ice cream over hard ice cream, I need to offer that option. Kids will be the ones who will be bringing their parents to my store. I realize that that decision makes good sense. What about combining crepes and ice cream? Including crepes as a part of Cherry Blossom will not require a lot of expensive new equipment. Commercial crepe-making machines are fairly inexpensive. I will already have adequate refrigeration space. Offering crepes will force me to add a dishwashing machine. It will also require me to have a coffee service. Staffing the store will also be different as an ice cream store can probably open a few hours later than one serving breakfast crepes. There is also a skill level that will be necessary to make great crepes. At the same time, utilizing the building and increasing the Cherry Blossom's revenue and at the same time maximizing my employees' skills has to be viewed as a positive. It is time to make a decision about the crepes. If they are to be added, then the store layout needs to be modified. Even the sign out front needs to be changed from Cherry Blossom Creamery to Cherry Blossom Creamery and Creperie.

Maybe it is time to visit a local creperie. I decided to take a trip to a fairly new establishment in Lebanon called Ancestor's Creperie. It is located in a small strip-style shopping center surrounded by new apartment buildings. The construction around it is still being completed. Once the apartments are finished and rented, it appears that there will be plenty of foot traffic. Even without those potential customers, I was pleasantly surprised by the number of customers enjoying the crepes.

My mission in this mini road trip was to evaluate how adding crepes as a major point of emphasis to my concept would affect the resulting space to be more or less in line with my mental picture of Cherry Blossom. The first item I noticed was the coffee service. There were dozens of flavors in bottles neatly displayed. The menu reflected their importance by listing lattes, chai, Macchiatos, and so many more.. The dining room was well-appointed with subdued wall colors and a tile-like floor. The crepes were made in plain view of the customer. This is something that I would do if I choose to make crepes. The crepes were served on attractive plates along with real silverware. There was even a busing tub for the customers to place their used plates and silverware. There was a relaxed vibe that customers tended to linger in. Posting of the free wifi password certainly reinforced that perception.

I had gathered information and impressions. It was time to make one of many important decisions. Although the products, ice cream and crepes, would play well with each other, I had serious reservations about how the customers of each would get along. I saw Cherry Blossom as a fun, at times frenetic, but also a laid-back place with bright colors, upbeat music, and enthusiastic and friendly staff. I saw kids running and shouting, particularly in our outdoor seating area, with abandon. I envisioned families and visitors posing at the stain glass mural. I understood that I could alter the vibe in how we served crepes, but it was going to be a struggle. I saw no way around using real dishes and silverware. I would definitely need a commercial dishwasher. I doubted that I could offer only a simple coffee service. I had little interest in serving specialty teas or coffees. A part of my concept involved serving people in a friendly, accurate and quick manner. I wanted customers to come often, but not linger. The model in my head was more in line with how a good pizza place operates, and not how a neighborhood coffee shop is run. It appeared to me that many times, successful businesses were able to do a fairly limited number of activities, but to do them well and then repeat them again and again.

It was with some blessed clarity that I began to really see Cherry Blossom Creamery. My vision for this business was becoming more defined. We would offer the best hard and soft ice cream we were capable of producing. The store would be brightly painted. The floors would shine. There would be a stain glass mural nearby. There would be music. Artwork would hang on the walls. Our staff would greet customers immediately with a genuine smile. The customers would be served quickly and accurately. Cherry Blossom Creamery would be that refuge from the rest of the retail world. We would push through the incompetence, inattentiveness, and unfriendliness that characterized so many other businesses. When our customer left Cherry Blossom Creamery, it would be with a smile and the firm intention of returning soon. I felt comfortable with my decision. Cherry Blossom would begin its existence as a Creamery without the attendant Creperie concept.

Chapter 2

Legally, starting any new business is a lot like unraveling a ball of knotted twine. There are so many things that need to be orchestrated, many of which need to be done almost simultaneously. There are permits that need to be obtained, whether they relate to building codes or to specific activities that the business is going to engage in. I had enough experience with starting a business to understand that I would need a license to collect sales tax. I would need to choose how the business was to be organized. In this case, I choose to have the business be an LLC. I contacted my lawyer and gave him the pertinent information, and he, with the aid of a check, registered Cherry Blossom Creamery as an LLC, which came with its own EIN number. With that done, I was able to open my commercial bank account and now even had checks with Cherry Blossom Creamery printed on them. I now had the ability to hire and pay employees, make sales, and send the appropriate taxes to Pennsylvania and the U S government. All of this I had done several times before. The small ball of twine looked a lot smoother, a lot more organized,

As I was staring at a business that was entirely new to me, there was a second, much more intimidating ball of legal twine. I needed to obtain permits for a frozen dessert license, a food establishment registration, a milk processing permit, and a retail food facility and restaurant license. At least those were the ones that I was aware of. Each of these applications had questions that were not possible to answer without other information that I had not yet gathered. On one application, it was necessary to detail employee hygiene and health standard operating procedures. Other questions included the square footage of our establishment. There were questions as to what would be on our menu, our number of employees, types of food we would serve. There were facility questions as to our lighting schedule, types of flooring, wall covering and equipment layout. Another application asked if we had a certified food manager on staff. What was that? I did a little research and found that it was a person who needed to have undergone training and passed a certification exam. This was a knot that maybe I could untangle.

I found a food safety course that was being held at the Berks County extension of Penn State. I paid my seventy-five dollars and arrived half an hour early for the all-day class. As we were in the middle of the COVID pandemic, the course was held in an outside pavilion. Instructors and students alike were dressed in winter coats while the wind whipped off the adjacent beautiful stream. We learned about time-sensitive foods that needed to be kept out of the temperature danger zone. We learned about proper cleaning and the mantra of wash, rinse, sanitize. We discussed the need for proper personal hygiene and hand washing. Proper storage of food and the need to prevent cross-contamination were introduced. The course was designed for a wide range of food preparation. Discussions related to the proper handling of meat, seafood, and most prepared foods did not apply to the food establishment that I was planning. I spent the time to learn those procedures as well as I needed to pass the exam that was administered at the same outdoor pavilion the following week. It was just as cold and windy on the day of the test as it was during the instructional portion of the course.

Following the exam, I met with a long-time friend at a nearby restaurant. Jim, like almost everyone else whom I had shared my desire to open an ice cream store with, was without much enthusiasm for this idea. He was only a few years younger than I and expressed how he had no desire to begin any venture that would consume this much of his time. There are so many good reasons not to do many things in life. It requires a stubborn nature not to allow others to keep you from doing those things. But sometimes, good-intentioned friends are right. I guess I would find out if I ever am able to open my store.

A few weeks later, I got the email that I had passed the exam and was now a certified food safety manager. This certification would last for five years. I could finally check one of the boxes on one of the applications.

I needed to distill the information from this course and make it my own. I wanted and needed the proper handling of food, the proper and safe serving of food, and the proper cleaning of our store to be a part of every employee's training. This was a new task that I needed to pursue. Parallel to the application process, I wanted to develop a food safety process for Cherry Blossom Creamery. I needed this to be part of the process. This would be the beginning of Cherry Blossom's standard operating procedures.

Chapter 3

There is no correct time order to solve the problems that are associated with beginning any type of business. There are so many questions, but many of the decisions that have to be made are based on the size of the property and its location. Finding the location for Cherry Blossom Creamery seemed like a good place to begin.

I thought finding and evaluating a location would be straightforward. I have lived in Hershey all my life and had an easy familiarity with foot and vehicular traffic. I hoped that this would allow me to properly evaluate different locations. My real estate agent, Molly, once she became aware of my desire to open an ice cream shop, began to bring possible sites to my attention.

The first one that we spent any time with was located in the center of town, one street from Chocolate Avenue. It had the proper commercial zoning and could be seen from Chocolate Avenue as long as you looked in the right direction. It had little off-street parking, but a parking lot across the street provided ample parking except for Sunday morning when the church filled the parking lot. Cherry Blossom Creamery did not plan to be open on Sunday mornings. The property did have a good-sized front porch, which would encourage outdoor seating, but it had no easy access to use the back yard for additional outdoor seating.

This property checked a lot of the right boxes. It had good visibility, decent parking, a bit of outdoor seating, and possibly enough room for producing the ice cream while still having some indoor seating. Unfortunately, the property was a wreck. Exterior renovations would include a new roof, new siding, and considerable work on the front porch. A significant handicap accessible ramp would, although not required, need to be built, as I felt that an ice cream store should be open to as many people as possible. That was going to be the easy part. The interior of the property had been divided into three rental opportunities. The second floor had been made into an apartment, which was accessed through a series of stairs off the back yard. On the side of the house, there was an office which had its own entrance in the front. The main portion of the house had the normal couple of bedrooms, one bath, a living room, and a kitchen. If we were to make this an ice cream store, possibly the bathroom and one of the bedrooms would remain as they were. Everything else would have to be gutted and rebuilt for ice cream production and the means to serve our customers. A few other issues also needed to be addressed. The front door would need to be moved as the stairs to the basement were too close to the existing opening and would cause a safety and aesthetic concern. Finally, the price of the property was such that the only way that paying the mortgage would be possible would be to retain the office and apartment as they were, as I would need them to help generate the revenue to pay the mortgage.

Even with all the concerns that I should have had with this property, it was more a reflection of my enthusiasm than my common sense that I still made an offer. The offer reflected some of the costs to correct structural issues, such as the roof and the siding. Molly presented the offer, and luckily, the owner rejected it and made no counteroffer. The owner eventually removed the property from the market. She made all the repairs that we had noted and retained the property as an investment property for herself. Looking back, I am grateful that I was saved from myself.

It was time to question if buying a property was the best course of action for Cherry Blossom Creamery. I had always felt that a business should be able to support the mortgage on the property where it was located. It was a principle that had been formed from a remnant of a conversation that I had had with a childhood friend. John Davis and I have been and still are very active tennis players. We had traveled in my old Chevy Impala to junior tournaments when I was barely old enough to drive. Long drives and sleeping in that car to avoid hotel bills that neither of us could afford had given us abundant time to discuss anything. John had mentioned on a couple of occasions that his father had believed that if nothing else good came out of one of his businesses, at least he would own and hopefully pay for the building where that business had been located.

Although John did not create many businesses of his own, he did take his father's advice about real estate and became a very successful developer and owner of many properties. My first few businesses were located in rental spaces, and once those businesses no longer existed, I had nothing tangible to show for my efforts. With that experience in mind, as I built new businesses, I purchased the properties where they were to be housed. Even with their demise, I was able to retain the real estate. That real estate was the basis for whatever wealth I had so far accumulated. That capital was what afforded me the opportunity to pursue this dream of an ice cream store. But was it the best idea to use so much of it to purchase a property? Maybe it was time for the business to be the creator of wealth and not have the creation of wealth be a byproduct of owning the real estate.

I had rented space decades ago in a ten-store strip mall in downtown Hershey. Hershey's downtown is a puzzle. A town that draws over four million tourists a year should have a vibrant, busy, and unique character. When I last rented space in Hershey's downtown, it was anything but vibrant or busy. Its character was unique. As a downtown, it did not exist. It began with what had been historically the town's department store, which was now an office building. Across the street was a large one-story building that housed a bank and a great pizza shop. As you continued beyond the pizza shop, the fire department building was next, followed by a large Methodist church. On the next block, there was finally something that appeared to be commercial. It was a long-established Italian-style restaurant and an assortment of small shops. Across the street from this were large two-story homes and a vacant lot the length of the entire block. The next block was home to a seven-story apartment building, and finally, the strip mall where I had once had my tennis and running shop located. The block across the street was a mix of residences and a few small shops or offices. As you ventured beyond my shop, there was a gas station, lumber yard and more homes. There were a few scattered businesses on the streets that ran on the south side of Chocolate Ave, on streets named Caracas or Granada. There was little pedestrian traffic for good reasons, as there was little to entice anyone to walk a fractured and uninviting downtown.

Thinking that I had located my tennis and running store in downtown Hershey, it bothered me when a tourist would innocently ask where downtown was located. I came to realize that anyone coming to my store was coming there as a destination and had not arrived on impulse from being drawn to our non-existent downtown. With that firmly in mind, when my lease expired, I purchased a property a mile east of the square, but still located on Chocolate Avenue and moved my store there. In the decades that had passed, Hershey had changed. There were still structural problems with the new downtown, but there were huge improvements. The old department store now housed two high-end and busy restaurants. There was a multi-level parking garage adjacent to a major tourist draw, the Hershey Story Museum. The old one-story bank and pizza shop had been demolished and replaced by a grassy vacant lot, which was not an improvement. The new, beautiful firehouse that had been constructed beside the Methodist Church did nothing to enhance the downtown vibe. Fortunately, the long-standing vacant lot across Chocolate Ave had been developed into a row of name restaurants and shops. Primati, Iron Hill Brewery, Freshido, Great Clips, First Watch, Starbucks and Tropical Café, among others, brought great numbers of patrons, locals and tourists alike to what was now a pedestrian-filled and vibrant two or three-block area of Hershey.

On one side of Chocolate Ave, there is a Chipotle restaurant that begins on the next block of the downtown area. On the opposite side of Chocolate Ave is that same seven-story apartment complex with a ten-story strip mall hugging the street. Continuing to walk past the strip mall, there is a free-standing and very busy Duck Donuts. It was in that ten-store shopping strip that I had once operated my sports shop. It was now where I was planning to begin Cherry Blossom Creamery.

One of the benefits of working with Rich at Love's Thermal Systems was that he offered to inspect this possible site for my store and give his feedback as to its potential success. He would also sketch the layout of the equipment for both the production and sale of the ice cream. Tim from Commercial Refrigeration combined with Rich to determine what would have to be added in the way of plumbing and electrical specifications to install my equipment. This would be a great help when enlisting the services of an architect to draw up the sealed plans that would be necessary for obtaining a building permit.

They met with me and both thought that this was a good location. The space had a lot in its favor. There was abundant electrical capability. The plumbing would be no more difficult than in most spaces. Rich promptly sent me a drawing with all of the equipment placed throughout the rental space.

It had been years since I had rented any significant space. It was true that I rented small areas that I used for storage, but those spaces had required little in the way of a lease or any long-term commitment on my part. Now I was negotiating a lease that would have a far-reaching impact on both the possibility of succeeding in this venture and how long I would be committed to its future. The actual lease was lengthy. There were clauses concerning operating hours and penalties for violating those dictates. There was a clause requiring reporting gross sales on a quarterly basis to the landlord. When I questioned those clauses, the leasing agent replied that I was leasing from a real estate development company that owned properties throughout the country and that the lease template that they were using served many different types of tenants and, therefore, there were clauses that did not apply to my location or type of business. He was more than happy to remove those particular clauses.

I was becoming a little less comfortable, but I continued to work on leasing in this location. My local contact was their apartment complex manager. She had been incredibly helpful with information and quick to return calls and e-mails. On numerous occasions, she had let me in to view the space by myself or with different contractors. If she were the owner of the property, I would have had much less hesitation in going forward. Instead, any final approvals had to go through the home office in Chicago. This increased the difficulty in working out details. More importantly, it removed the personal relationship that I always valued.

It was time to negotiate. I wanted a two-year lease with options to renew for an additional four years. I also wanted free rent for six months while I did the build-out. If I were able to open earlier than six months, I would add additional months to the beginning of the lease and pay the rate that we would agree to for the first year of the lease. I did not want the rent to increase during the first two years, but I realized that I would expect an increase in rent for that additional four-year option. I wanted it to be 1 percent. Several weeks would pass before the landlord and I had a final lease for me to sign.

The final lease was a major compromise. It had three months free for my build-out. I did not need to worry that I would be open before that period ended, as I fully expected it to take four to eight months to get ready to open. The lease was now structured as a three-year lease with one three-year option. Rent increased each year by two percent. That modest increase would result in rent beginning at $1750.00 a month and by the sixth year, it would increase to $1932.14. The lease arrived by overnight mail. It was now my job to take it to a notary and sign it. Then it needed to be sent back with a check for the security deposit and the first month's rent.

I took the lease to a notary and had her witness my signing of the lease. I was ready to take it to the UPS store and send it on its way, but I began to have second thoughts. Traveling to my landscape clients, I passed by my hoped-for location several times daily. Cars with tourists were plentiful and made for a slow go, but pedestrian traffic decreased markedly by the time they would have reached my proposed location. There were lots of pedestrians in the preceding block, but there didn't seem to be enough stores or restaurants in my block to draw them past my new store.

I reasoned that this might not be a big problem. Some of the ice cream stores that I patronize are not within walking distance. They are destination shops. You drove to them. This location had tons of parking. This location had good visibility. People should see it and park their cars, and buy my ice cream. Once again, I became hesitant. The plentiful parking in the rear of the store made it necessary for anyone wishing to purchase an ice cream cone to walk from the parking lot all the way around the building and enter my front door. There was a rear entrance, but it was only used by the tenants as it was a shared space that was accessed by climbing several stairs.

I grew more concerned and less confident about my location. I left the rear parking lot and attempted to turn left onto Chocolate Ave. It wasn't even morning or evening rush hour, but it still took several minutes and a bit of courage to finally make that left turn. I made that left turn and thought to myself, "Would I come to get ice cream very often from this location? Would I fight the tourist-filled traffic of Chocolate Ave to get to my location, then turn into the rear parking lot? Would I then walk all the way around the building to make my purchase and then once again walk all the way around the building to get to my car, which I would sit in for several minutes before getting out onto Chocolate Ave?" The more I thought about this second possible location, the more I began to realize that my enthusiasm to begin Cherry Blossom Creamery had made me blind to some challenging issues with this location. After a day had passed, I still felt that this was not the right spot for me. I called the leasing agent and apologized for the wasted effort and time that he had spent, but I was not ready to move forward. The search would continue.

As I had previously mentioned in 1984, when I was the owner of a sporting goods store, called The Best Choice, I had purchased a property on the east end of Hershey, right on Chocolate Ave. The more I searched for possible locations, the more I became convinced that I might just own the right spot. Currently, a boutique wine maker, Cullari Winery, was renting the space I had in mind. The space was the appropriate size. It was just under sixteen hundred square feet. It stood by itself with plenty of parking both in the front and back of the store. I had constructed a beautiful back patio that featured a stunning fountain. Over the years, I had planted beautiful and interesting shrubs, perennials, annuals and bulbs in the gardens to the front and side of the location. The inside of the building was a split level. The bottom portion had hardwood floors. This space would be where the ice cream would be dipped, and the soft ice cream would be served. One accessed the upper level in two easy steps. This would be the area where the production room would be located. There was also room for twenty-four seats. On both levels, it would be possible to display other items in addition to ice cream.

The only problem was that Sal Cullari, the owner, had been leasing this space since 2007, which was almost fourteen years. Sal was an excellent tenant. He kept the property looking great. He paid his rent on time. Over the years, we had gotten to know each other, and we got along fine. What he had not done was to make a commitment to a long-term lease. In fact, when his initial lease expired in 2011, he would not sign a new lease. He wished for our agreement to run as a month-to-month lease, which would allow either of us to terminate the lease with a written thirty-day notice. His reasoning was that he, being in his sixties, did not know how long he wanted to remain in this business or at least at this location. It was time to have a difficult conversation.

I told Sal that I wanted to open an ice cream store. Since we were all but the same age, he thought my idea to be less than sound. I disagreed and then told him the bad portion of why we were getting together. I explained that I wanted to open that store in the space that he was currently leasing. I explained that I had on numerous occasions requested that he enter into a multi-year lease. He had never wanted to do that. Sal knew that I could ask him to vacate in the next month. I also knew that I respected what Sal had done as a tenant, and I did not want to cause him undue hardship. I asked him what length of time would seem fair to him. After a bit of hesitation, he offered a time period of two years. I countered with a period of one year. As a compromise, we agreed on eighteen months. That would result in my location being empty and ready for me to begin work on it in December 2022. This would put my hoped-for opening date to be February 2023. When you are already seventy years old, this does appear to be risky long-term planning. I comforted myself by noting just how much needed to be done prior to opening. Most importantly, I pledged that I would use that time to prepare for this business to be unlike any other I had started. I would develop the standard operating procedures that I would need so that Cherry Blossom Creamery would be a prototype store. A store that could be reproduced. A store that could run itself. This would be a business that offered refuge from the rest of the world that happened to sell ice cream and a few other things. It wasn't an ice cream store; it was a business that sold ice cream. I would work on my business and not so much in it. This was heady stuff. It was terrifying.

CHAPTER 4

Waking in the middle of the night is a price that one pays for having reached one's seventh decade on earth. Many times, that awakening is preceded by dreams. Since I have decided to bring Cherry Blossom Creamery into being, the dreams have taken on new intensity. Last night, I had a dream about a venture that I had embarked upon called Tennis Buying Consultants. Two of us, Liz and I, proposed to simplify buying women's tennis apparel by breaking down the characteristics of each piece. If this were done so the inventory would not repeat itself, and the buyer could offer greater variety while not spending more buying dollars. At that time, I owned a tennis sporting goods store and had purchased a fair amount of women's tennis apparel. This was an activity that almost always resulted in many pieces of clothing being deeply discounted or items languishing on the racks. I thought that by discovering the characteristics that made the clothing different from each other, we could find a method for effectively purchasing women's tennis apparel. We rolled this concept out in 1979. Although we were unaware of it at the time, it was an attempt at discovering an algorithm for purchasing tennis apparel.

Tennis Buying Consultants floundered. We never discovered the algorithm, and quite possibly there was none to be found. Even if we had new styles that were continuously introduced, and would have defeated our attempts. What I do remember is the enthusiasm we pursued our goals. What I had recalled in my dream last night was our several trips to New York City and our meetings with some of the actual manufacturers of the tennis apparel. Liz and I were and are small-town people. Remembering that we took the risk and had the guts to follow through with traveling to the really big city has made me question why that subject was explored last night. Is it to encourage me? Is it to warn me that even with guts and a concept, often a project ends in failure?

The middle of the night is not a good time to evaluate a new or any venture. Did I have as many doubts about the other large financial decisions I had made throughout my life? Did I lose sleep when I purchased the property, which I have now owned for the last thirty years and will be the home to Cherry Blossom Creamery? In retrospect, I sure should have. In subsequent years, this property took much of my time and almost all my energy. Did I lose sleep when I started my landscape company? Not so much. I mistakenly thought I had the skills necessary to make it succeed. Only later did I realize just how much more I needed to learn. Is it from those experiences that are making me more hesitant in pursuing this venture? I know it will require me to learn whole new skill sets. I don't know how to make ice cream. I don't know how to operate a food establishment with all of its safety and regulatory oversights. The necessity to acquire those new skills is what I said I wanted. I do not wish to totally repeat myself. If this is my last chapter, I want it to be a new one.

During the day, all of these doubts are kept at bay. Three thirty in the morning is a different matter. This experience cannot be unique to me. Does everyone who wants to bring something new into being have to battle these questions and doubts?

Chapter 5

With the location for Cherry Blossom Creamery settled upon, I began to work on three segments of getting this business up and running. I needed to apply for a building permit. I needed to continue learning how to make ice cream. I needed to work through the permitting process I would need from the state to manufacture and sell my ice cream. All three needed to be accomplished. It felt like all three needed to be done at once.

The third segment that I needed to pursue was obtaining the appropriate permits from the Pennsylvania Department of Agriculture. Hours that I will never get back were spent researching what I would need. At first glance, it appeared that I needed to obtain a frozen dessert license, which made sense. Then, if I wanted to have the ability to sell wholesale, I would need a license to sell milk products. Initially, I thought I would also need a retail food and restaurant license. I contacted the appropriate people listed for Dauphin County and began asking questions in the hope that I might be able to complete an application. All were there to answer my questions, but they indicated that I needed to wait until I had my concept more refined as to what I wanted to sell other than ice cream. I would also need equipment lists and lighting layout, and wall coverings. None of which I was ready to document. It was mid-June 2021, which was well over a year from my taking possession of the store. This permitting process would need to be delayed until I had more information.

Building permits in our township are good for one year after they are issued. By the time I find an architect and have sealed drawings done, the seventeen months I had to get this accomplished will have diminished considerably. The first step was finding an architect during the time of COVID. Initially, I contacted a local builder, Hartman Home Improvements. I had seen some of their work and thought it to be excellent. My meeting at their office went well. Barry Hartman and their architect, Frank, made a site visit the following week. I had assembled other architectural drawings that I had had made when we converted my prospective rental space from a residence to its present commercial status. I also gave them all the specifications that I had for the equipment that would be installed in the space.

A few weeks passed, and I had not heard anything from Frank. A few e-mails later, he apologetically informed me that not only was he having difficulty finding an electrical engineer, but he had also become sick. He offered to return the materials that I had given him. He could not commit to a time frame for finishing this job. I reluctantly stopped by his house, where his wife returned my documents.

Realizing that I did have a fair amount of time to obtain that building permit and not being sure exactly who to call next, I decided to concentrate on one of the other segments. I had registered for an ice cream seminar that Malcolm Stogo was holding.

This would be a two-day hands-on opportunity to observe and participate in making ice cream, gelato, sorbets, and some ice cream novelties. The seminar was held in West Orange, New Jersey.

Prior to even knowing where I was going to put my ice cream store or even if I was going to actually go forward with this idea, I had taken an online seminar with Malcolm. This was January 2020, and COVID had forced Malcolm to not offer in-person seminars but instead Zoom meetings. I watched for four hours as he and his assistant demonstrated how to use the batch freezer. They showed how to assemble the clean parts in the morning, then make ice cream, then change flavors, and finally, the end-of-day clean up. It was not the fault of the class, but I just disappear when I am on a Zoom meeting. I barely said a word. At the conclusion of the four hours, I left with the impression that this was a doable concept, but one that I needed a lot more help with. One of the benefits of taking this online course was that Malcolm made himself available to answer any questions over the next month. I did take advantage of that.

Now I was going to have the opportunity to get up close and personal with the art of making ice cream. I arrived the night before the seminar and stayed at a nationally known brand hotel. After registering and paying a non-reduced room rate, I was informed that, because of COVID, the swimming pool, the exercise gym, the bar, and the restaurant were closed. My room would only be cleaned if I requested it. My bed sheets would be changed if I let them know of that desire. Fortunately, the cable still functioned for the television, and I settled in for the evening.

The next morning, I was both excited and a bit apprehensive. On one hand, I knew I never did well when I was learning something while being observed. It was one of the reasons why tennis was such a good fit for me. I could go off by myself and work on my serve, or my toss for the serve, or hit balls against a wall. This allowed me the freedom to fail in front of only myself while I was learning a new skill. I was also worried about finding the location for the seminar. On the other hand, I needed to see if this ice cream business was for me.

Although the seminar did not begin until nine in the morning, I left my hotel at eight and followed the GPS to the given address. I had expected to see a commercial building with Ice Cream University emblazoned on its side. What I saw was a beautiful house on a large, lavishly landscaped lot in a very upscale neighborhood. I was getting nervous. I rechecked the address. It appeared that I had found the right address. With no other option, I called the phone number that I had. Once I established that the person answering the phone was Malcolm, I explained my concern. He assured me that I was at the correct address, but that the seminar did not begin for another forty-five minutes, and I could come back closer to nine o'clock.

I returned close to nine o'clock and noticed a young man standing outside the front door with a suitcase. I parked my car and walked to the front door. He appeared pleased to see me, as he was as confused as I had been just forty-five minutes earlier. He had taken an Uber from LaGuardia and had just arrived at the same unlikely destination for an ice cream seminar as I had forty-five minutes earlier. After introductions, I told him that I had talked with Malcolm earlier and that we were at the right place. By this time, the door was opened, and we were greeted by our host.

Malcolm is a thin, slightly stooped man in his late seventies. We were led through a beautiful house decorated with fine paintings and an abundance of plants as we headed to the basement. I thought we might wait for the other participants in our seminar, but Malcolm informed Tim and me that we were the only two. COVID had reduced the number of willing travelers, and Malcolm was also limiting the number to two or three to minimize close contact. Once we saw the basement area, I had a better understanding. It was a commercial kitchen complete with an appropriate three-compartment sink, bathroom, two small batch freezers, a pasteurizer, blender, induction range, work tables, refrigerator, and shelving. Even for the four of us, Malcolm, his assistant, Tim and I, it was a tight fit.

We immediately began to make ice cream. Soon, we were adding ice cream mix, two-fold vanilla extract, vanilla specks, and pasteurized egg yolks into the batch freezer. We turned on the dasher, set the timer, turned on the refrigeration, and began our first batch. Ten minutes later, we extruded the finished product. For the ice cream to be finished, it needs to have the proper consistency. The ice cream needed to be "wavy," making it able to stand up on the spatula while still being soft. The ice cream is quickly packaged into pint containers, which are turned upside down and placed in the freezer.

The next batch continued using vanilla as a base but added chocolate chips. We needed to properly melt the chocolate wafers in a double boiler. All of the ingredients except half of the chocolate chips and the liquid chocolate were poured into the batch freezer. The timer was set to eight minutes, and refrigeration was turned on. When the batch was complete, the second half of the chocolate chips and the melted chocolate were added. The refrigeration was turned off, and the finished product was extruded. The packed pints had their tops decorated with chocolate chips and then turned upside down and placed in the freezer. It was important to pack the ice cream as quickly as possible. Exposure to warm air would lead to the formation of ice crystals. Every attempt is made to minimize this from happening, which is why a hardening cabinet, which has a temperature of minus 40 degrees Fahrenheit, is essential in order to make great ice cream.

Malcom did not have a hardening cabinet. He instead used a standard chest freezer. Since he would not be selling any of this ice cream, but instead giving it away, he had no need for this expensive and very heavy piece of equipment.

The morning continued as we made cookie monster, chocolate, coffee, and strawberry ice cream. We learned about marinating the frozen strawberries. We learned the importance of fresh lemon juice in enhancing the flavor of fruit-based ice creams.

After standing all morning, a break for lunch was most welcome. We adjourned to Malcolm's dining room. DoorDash had delivered our selections. Now, five of us, including Malcolm's wife, joined us sat down for a leisurely lunch. The discussion centered around what Tim and I hoped to accomplish with ice cream. We also learned of some of Malcolm's past endeavors as well as some stories from his work as an ice cream consultant.

The afternoon followed much as the morning had. New flavors continued to be produced, such as strawberry cheesecake, ricotta fig, and a liquor-based ice cream that I cannot now recall. When we finished the afternoon, I was tired, my back hurt from all day standing, and I was less certain that this ice cream business was for me.

The next day, we were slow to rush to the basement. Instead, we spent time in Malcolm's living room, where he made himself available to answer any of our questions that he might have had from the first day. He further explored our plan for whatever we were going to do with our ice cream business.

Once we returned to the basement, we began making some gelatos. We then did a few sorbets and even some Italian ice. This was interesting, but I did not see those products as at least initially being offered in Cherry Blossom Creamery. What we did make that I had been waiting for was two flavors of plant-based, lactose-free ice cream. This was a niche that I wanted Cherry Blossom Creamery to exploit. I wanted to make great, creamy, delicious lactose-free flavors that we would make available in our dipping case as well as our display freezer. Once I tasted what we had made during the afternoon, I was certain that we could offer a great lactose-free ice cream. Only after actually producing these plant-based flavors would I learn how solid they would freeze. This would not allow us to have the dairy-free flavors in our dipping cases, as they were all but impossible to dip. Other ways needed to be found to allow us to offer single servings of dairy-free ice cream to our customers. The final item we made was ice cream pops. These required a mold and popsicle sticks. With the proper wrapping, I could see these as an important product in our store.

The seminar was over, but maybe the best part for me was yet to come. Malcolm insisted that I pick out as many pints of ice cream that we had just made and take them with me. Tim was flying back to Los Angeles, making it impossible for him to take any of the ice cream. I had purchased several Stay Cold bags at the neighboring grocery store. I was more than willing and now ready to bring home a good selection of what we had done the last two days. When I was leaving, I still had serious misgivings as to whether making ice cream was really for me. I didn't know if I had the physical stamina to produce enough ice cream for this to be worthwhile. I didn't know if I was ready to devote so much of my time to this endeavor.

My attitude changed once I got home. I gave several flavors to four of my friends. The lactose-free was handed out as well. I did keep five or six pints for Sue and me. The feedback was incredible. My lactose-intolerant friend said, "That chocolate is so good, it is the only chocolate you need to make." Obviously, he did not find a lactose-free ice cream to be a compromise. Other friends raved about the flavor and creaminess. Sue and I could do nothing but smile while we were eating the ice cream that we had kept. This ice cream was really good. I didn't know if it was so good because it was so fresh or if Malcolm was so gifted at making ice cream. I was hoping that I could duplicate what we were eating.

The production of this great ice cream had become more than a business opportunity. I realized that this ice cream needed to come into existence. It needed to be available in Hershey, my hometown, a place that I truly loved. It was now my mission to produce this ice cream. I also knew that making great ice cream would not be enough. I still needed to create a great business to go with it.

Such a conflicting set of emotions. The quote for a sizable portion of the large equipment necessary to open Cherry Blossom Creamery is sitting on my desk. At once it is too large a number, and at the same time it feels like it is too small a number. The sense that it is too large a number is easy to understand. Money is always difficult to put at risk. The money that you spent several years earning and saving now being lumped together and sent on its way to fund an adventure that has no certain happy ending. That is the easiest emotion to identify—fear. Is this the correct use of this accumulated wealth?

The other emotion is much more slippery. Thinking that the number is too small takes more thought.

Is this adventure large enough? Is it possible that what I am going to burden myself with is too small an enterprise, and I realize belatedly that this risk was too pedestrian? It is always possible to make more money, but it is never possible to regain the time that one has used. Will I be wasting too much of mine? Is the dream too small? Bringing an ice cream store into existence does not feel very unique. There are thousands of ice cream stores. What can I do with this dream that will have been worth the journey? This emotion is trickier—possibly regret, apprehension, or doubt. What it is not at this moment is joy. Even if I can reach the goals I have set for this ice cream store, will the gem that I create be so small that it will not have been worth the effort?

If this store is to be manifested, then I have to sign the proposal and send the appropriate money to the refrigeration company. If I am going to equip my test kitchen, I will need a blast freezer, some refrigeration, a three-bay sink, and a batch ice cream freezer. The other items, including a hand sink, a display freezer, a three-door refrigerator, a bain marie, and two different-sized dipping cabinets, could wait. Our proposed opening is not for a year from this date, but COVID and its attendant supply chain problems have dictated that it would be smart to forestall the anticipated price increases and remove the issue of long delays by purchasing and paying for all of those items today.

It has taken several tries to come up with where I am going to install my test kitchen. I strongly felt that one of the first hurdles that I needed to remove for making this venture a success was my lack of knowledge as to how to make ice cream. I purchased books, have taken a virtual seminar and even a hands-on seminar, but I still have no confidence in the ability to produce the high-quality ice cream I so needed to not just make this a success but also to make it a store I could take pride in. The test kitchen would be a place where I could fail, by myself, and try again. It had always been my pattern that I needed to learn new skills alone. I was terrible at having an instructor or a coach, no matter how great they were. As I have aged, I am a bit better at taking instruction, but I still draw into myself and do not get the true benefit from someone else's direction.

A test kitchen would also force me to search out the resources that I would need to produce my ice cream. I would need to purchase double-fold vanilla, high-grade chocolate, frozen and possibly fresh fruit, peanut butter, stabilizers, milk, eggs, cream, and so much more. If I were producing even small amounts of ice cream, I would need to establish relationships with many suppliers. That would be essential when producing enough ice cream for the store.

Chapter 6

It was the beginning of December 2021, and what had seemed like a very long time to develop an ice cream store now loomed much closer. I would have my space in less than a year. It was time to get those plans finalized with an architect's seal on them. I had discovered an architectural firm located in Wernersville while driving to a friend's house in Reading. Their sign said that they were a design studio complete with the appropriate electrical and plumbing engineers on staff. I stopped in, met with Chuck, discussed what I was planning, and he assured me that their firm could handle the building permit process.

He forwarded a service agreement, which I returned signed to him. The first step was a visit to our site. That is when that visit made me uncomfortable. I had asked him to explore with me a way to make my store more handicap accessible. Currently, it had a rather narrow, softly curved ramp from the back parking lot into the back door. It was a little too steep and maybe too narrow to properly accommodate a wheelchair. This was what had been approved twenty years ago when this space had been converted from a single residence to a commercial space. I truly want to improve this in a way to have the accessibility necessary to allow anyone to eat the best ice cream ever. Chuck understood my desire, but he was not so certain that I could do much to improve my situation. Even worse, he was concerned that I might have to spend a lot of money and change a lot of things for Cherry Blossom Creamery to get a building permit issued. He suggested that I contact the accessibility code enforcement officer and try to get him to visit the site to determine just what I would need to do. He wanted this done before he spent more time on my plans.

I had not considered the possibility that this space would not meet the requirements necessary for me to use it as my ice cream store. It was a wine tasting and wine selling store. I was only changing the product. Now it was an ice cream tasting and ice cream selling store. What was I to do? Of course, I contacted the enforcement officer. As I waited for a meeting with him, I was on edge. I had already ordered much of my equipment. I had sent a check for almost sixty thousand dollars to Tim. I had sent ten thousand dollars to Rich. I had ordered a seven-thousand-dollar machine from Malcolm. I was committed. I had told Sal that he needed to be out of the property in twelve months. If this space was not going to work out, I was very uncertain what I would do. If I were not able to make the necessary adjustments to the property, not only would I not be able to use this space, but even worse, this property, which I owned, would not be able to be rented to anyone. When Sal moved out, I would not have a viable rental space.

I was truly going down the proverbial rabbit hole. I was informed in an email that Derry Township did not have the right to override the Pennsylvania Department of Labor and Industry as to accessibility requirements. Derry Township's community development director suggested that if I had a sketch, he would be able to meet with me and my architect to give some guidance. Until today, I had made the assumption that since the existing winery had an occupancy permit, I would not be dealing with any other governmental agency other than Derry Township. I had owned this commercial property for thirty-seven years and had done significant renovations. All of those renovations required me to deal with Labor and Industry. It was always difficult and had often required a third party that knew how to navigate the application and approval process. In these COVID times, no one wanted to take personal meetings. I was left communicating by passing emails. Often, the question that I needed answered was either ignored, misinterpreted, or I had asked the wrong question. I wasn't sure that a face-to-face meeting would help, but I decided that was what I wanted. That next day, the Board of Supervisors was having its biweekly meeting. I knew that the community development director, Chuck, was normally in attendance. This was a public meeting. My ambush was planned. I am not attempting to confuse you, the reader, but both my architect and the community development director are named Chuck. What are the odds?

I did attend the public township supervisors meeting and had the opportunity to speak with Chuck. He informed me that the enforcement code had been updated since the winery had been granted an occupancy. He was certain that with this change, the accessibility issue was once again opened. Chuck thought it would be helpful for me to work with his assistant, Darrin. Not what I had hoped for. I still had no direction. Should I submit a building permit application that would be rejected? Should I have my architect aid me in filing a variance with Labor and Industry? I was stuck.

The next morning, I decided to return to the township offices and try to spend some time with Darrin. Fortunately, he was available, and he spent a good amount of time pulling all of the permits for this property. After a lot of searching, it became apparent that when the winery filed for its occupancy permit, the usage was changed from B, business, to M, mercantile. The township was now forcing me to change usage back to business, as Cherry Blossom was viewed more like a restaurant than a retail shop. Any argument that I presented was not met with acceptance.

Both Chuck, who had stopped by while Darrin and I were discussing this situation, and Darrin felt that there was almost no way to comply with the access as required by current building codes. They advised me that Labor and Industry were normally understanding about cost and feasibility when it related to older buildings. As much as I was frustrated with what could only be thought of as a setback, I now had direction.

I contacted Chuck, the architect, related what had transpired and asked him to go forward with drawing the plans. We thought it best that once the plans were drawn that they be forwarded to our electrical, plumbing, and carpentry contractors so that they could price out the renovations required. There is a rule that is commonly adhered to by Labor and Industry that no more than twenty percent of the cost of the remodel should be spent addressing the accessibility issue. I needed my contractors to sharpen their pencils. I had no objection to spending some money to make my ice cream store more accessible, but I did not want to completely ruin the beauty of my location by having ugly ramps complete with multiple switchbacks. Most importantly, I did not want to have to address the two steps that separated the dipping area from the seating area. Anyone who gained access from the rear would be more than adequately served by our staff, making navigating those two steps a non-issue. If twenty percent of the renovation could be kept modest, then neither multiple ramps nor revisions to the different levels of the store would be possible, as the cost would far exceed the twenty percent rule.

Chapter 7

Taking stock

After what has been a dispiriting and frustrating two weeks, I thought I needed to take stock of what has been accomplished and what still needs to be done. It is mid-December, and less than a year until I take possession of the rental space that is to be Cherry Blossom Creamery. I have taken care of some basic items, including registering my name, obtaining my federal EIN number, opening a checking account, and securing a charge card in Cherry Blossom's name. I have found and decided on my location. I have determined that February 2023 is my opening date. I have attended two ice cream-making seminars. Armed with that knowledge, I have ordered almost all of the equipment that I will need to open. The plumbing and most of the electrical work have been done in my test kitchen. It only awaits a sink and the batch freezer to allow me to begin to make ice cream, if not for sale, to at least give away to friends.

I have explored other products that could be added to the ice cream store. I have made my first doggie ice cream. It is now being taste-tested by various dogs of my acquaintance. I am refining the crackers that everyone seems to love, which I am calling Pappy crackers. There is still work to do, but I am not too worried. I continue to work on the proper recipe for meadow tea and the method to produce it at the store and not in my home. The test kitchen will help out here. None of these products has proper packaging. A lot of work is ahead of me to get that done.

Much of the anxiety that I had experienced a few months ago concerning the building of an ice cream store has gone away. I am so much more certain that this is a business that can succeed and be one that I will enjoy. Some of the angst that I had felt was due to having to ask my long-time tenant, Sal, to end his lease as a winery. He has been extremely professional and has at least hidden any hostile feelings that he might have about this situation. That has gone a long way to lightening the guilt that I had been carrying with me.

Most blessedly, my general health has been excellent. This is not something that anybody should take for granted, but especially someone approaching seventy-two years of age. Writing this book and opening my store have given me a mental boost. I look forward to working on both when I come awake early in the morning.

Now to what isn't done. Most importantly, I do not have a building permit for my rental space. Because of the accessibility issues, my architect cannot, at this moment, do sealed drawings. Without that plan, it is almost impossible to complete the various state license applications.

I can only imagine how discouraged someone about to begin a new venture would be if they encountered the above obstacles and were not armed with experience and the time to work through the problems. How many great concepts have never been brought forth because the creator gave up or ran out of time? This book is by no means a how-to guide. It is meant to be a travelogue of how one person, me, has attempted to formulate a concept and then guide its creation to what is hoped to be a happy ending. This book hopes to be a window into how one entrepreneur is living through the business creating process. I hope to be honest in my frustrations, fears, and hopes for this business. It is also a narrative describing how I want this to be a different kind of business. I want it to be a small business that is self-sustaining. Creating a business that operates to fulfill my desires while at the same time fulfills the needs of my customers.

To that end, there is a lot to do. I have begun writing the standard operating procedures. I realize that with every new piece of equipment, I need to detail how it is to be operated. I need to demonstrate how to best use the equipment to maximize efficiency. I need to detail how to maintain and clean it. With each new item that we produce, whether it be each flavor of ice cream, doggie ice cream, meadow tea, or any other product we make, the recipe and procedure need to be written. These recipes have to be consistently followed.

It is vital that I begin the process of imaging this company. This is so extremely important if this is to be the company that I desire; it needs an organizational chart detailing all the jobs that need to be done. I need a Chief Operating Officer, a Chief Financial Officer, a vice president of marketing, a vice president of operations, and a human resources manager. Reporting to these are sales associates, the health compliance officer, the social media director, and the research and development director.

How am I going to afford to hire all of these people while selling four-dollar ice cream cones? I can't. I realize that initially, I will be doing all of these jobs. My goal has to be to organize and document the work that I do in each position so well that it will allow someone else to take over my job. I need to have lucid enough operational methods combined with well-thought-out training to find replacements for me in each of my many jobs.

Here at the Cherry Blossom Creamery's creation, there are a few other essential tasks that I need to complete. I need to use my best guess to determine a profit and loss statement as well as a cash flow analysis. Throughout the development of our products, I constantly need to record the costs of the ingredients that we use. I will need to record the time it takes to do the differing tasks that are required to produce each product. This will allow proper pricing of our products. At some point, it is necessary to locate attractive and affordable packaging for our many products.

Since I do not yet have a fully functional test kitchen, nor do I have the sealed plans that I need to construct Cherry Blossom, I need to use this time to organize this business. This is not the work that makes me very excited, as I have always been focused on the product and not on the process. I need to adjust my thinking. I need to get as excited about building a business as I am about making great ice cream.

Chapter 8

The last few weeks have been both productive and very troubling. On the plus side, I have good preliminary drawings from Chuck that will allow me to get cost estimates for the electrical, plumbing, and carpentry portions of the build-out for the store. I am scheduled to meet with all three contractors next week. Hopefully, we will have what we need to begin the Labor and Industry variance hearing very soon.

The sink is installed in the test kitchen. All that remains to outfit the test kitchen is the small batch freezer, which is ordered and is scheduled to arrive in the next few weeks. Learning to make ice cream is getting closer.

My work on the employee manual is provisionally complete. There will be a few revisions, but I feel that there is a strong foundation to that manual.

After some research, I happened upon an ice cream trade show. It is entitled the Great Lakes Ice Cream and Fast Food Show. It takes place in Battle Creek, Michigan, next week. Once quickly registered, and weather willing, I will be attending my first ice cream trade show. I made a list of some of the many items I haven't yet sourced, as well as questions that I might find answers to at this show. I must make myself ask even the really dumb questions. I have quite a few of them.

Now to the really troubling event of last week. A local pizza restaurant closed its doors six months ago. It is located on Main Street in Palmyra. Main Street is an extension to the east of my street, Chocolate Avenue. It is about one-half mile from my proposed store. My brother-in-law is a construction guy who is always interested in whatever he observes being built. He stopped and inquired as to what was going to occupy that real estate. They informed him that half of the building would continue to be a pizza place, but the other half would be an ice cream parlor. The ice cream would be hand-made by the Amish folks who were opening in April.

I don't know what to do. So much is rattling about in my head. I have spent a considerable amount of money on equipment that I will soon see arriving to be stored until December. Their new store will already have been open for nine months before I unpack my dipping cabinets, freezers, refrigerators, and all the other equipment I have purchased. Is there anywhere near enough business for two handmade ice cream shops within one mile of each other? I am in a state of panic.

I am certain that my shop will be different. Our store will proudly demonstrate how ice cream is made with our see-through glass doors. I doubt that they will do this. I know that our outdoor seating, as well as our gardens and lights, will be much more attractive and pleasing than what they can offer. I know our parking is better. I know that it is easier to get in and out of our parking lot than what they will face. Most importantly, I believe that if I can build Cherry Blossom Creamery in the manner that I am attempting, it will be a different kind of business than what I have ever built or most likely what my new competitor will attempt. The overriding question is, if I do make Cherry Blossom Creamery the business I want it to be, will my customers notice the difference and show it enough support, even with strong competition or will all this end in failure?

I would like to dissect this with my wife, Sue, but as of yet, I have not told her of this new development. During the forty-three years we have been married, I have begun several businesses and discussed many more possible ones with Sue. Until this ice cream venture, Sue has been open and supportive of almost anything that I dreamed of. This time, not so much. I think I understand her reticence. We are old, and when she looks at our friends, almost all of them are retired. Some are traveling. Some are spending all their winters in Florida. Many are volunteering. Most are spending time with their grandchildren. None of them is beginning new businesses. Sue is worried that we will miss out on some great opportunities to travel or on family time. In the back of her mind is the concern that, should I die or become too ill to do this venture, she will be stuck with a business she has no interest in operating. It will just be more complications to join the complications of the rental properties that we own.

As to the question of complications, the idea that once one has reached some arbitrary number of years on this earth, it is no longer reasonable to begin projects that may become messy if you are not there to see them through is extremely limiting. One of the things that my dad taught me that I value above almost everything else was his attitude on how to die. He was seventy-two. He had been diagnosed with a failing heart. One so fragile that even doing a bypass or other intervention was considered vastly unsafe. His cardiologist explained to my dad that he needed to enjoy the few good days that were left and endure the bad ones. He and I had a garden that we shared. It was early October, and without informing me, he had my brother-in-law go out to that garden and rototill it so that it would be ready for next spring's planting. He knew that there was almost no likelihood that he would see spring. Even if by some crazy chance he did, he would be in no shape to work in a garden. With all that, he looked to the future and prepared for it. That is so much better than giving up. He died in mid-October.

I would like to discuss this with my best friend, Bruce, but again, I hesitate. Bruce is my age and has operated a successful landscape business. He had significant real estate holdings, which he has at this moment cashed out of. He is a very sharp business person, but he is already convinced that maybe I should not pursue this venture. Bruce is thrilled that I will be producing great lactose-free ice cream that he will purchase, but he agrees with Sue that I am demonstrating a decided lack of judgment in starting this business. He views my participation in the ice cream business to be fraught with difficulties, the largest one being the ability to find employees. He predicts that I will be spending all of my time at the store.

The discovery of this close-by competition will strengthen both Sue's and Bruce's conviction that Cherry Blossom Creamery should be abandoned. There are always naysayers anytime that something new is looking to be created. How many times have prospective business originators given up in part because of comments from those closest to them? For the moment, I will not be discussing this with either Sue or Bruce.

Instead, I talked with one of my tenants who operates a very successful consignment clothing store. She assured me that with appropriate social media, we can drive enough customers to my store. She has been extremely active doing just that for her store. She also pointed out some of the advantages that we possess over the competitor's location, which I had also thought of. From our discussion, it is clear that she desires Cherry Blossom Creamery to open in our proposed location, which is right beside her store.

By chance, I walked by an open door of another of my tenants who specializes in massages and wedding ceremonies. She was sitting with a third tenant who does permanent makeup. I mentioned my unwelcome discovery. They were very encouraging. They astutely reasoned that I would have the advantage of seeing what kind of ice cream store my new competition brought forth. I would then be able to build a store that was different and better. Most importantly, they did not think that this was a death blow to my idea. We can only hope that they are correct. It is my intention not to change a thing from my vision, but to move forward with determination and carry a bit more worry.

Chapter 9

It is late January 2022, a bit over one year from opening the store and two years into attempting to bring Cherry Blossom Creamery alive. When I first envisioned an ice cream store, it was all very simple. I wanted to create the best ice cream possible. I was totally invested in the product creation, not so much in how this would turn into an ongoing business. I was excited about how the equipment would take an ice cream mix and blend that mix with other sumptuous ingredients to manufacture great, innovative flavors that would illicit "wow" as a response.

I quickly realized that in order to have anyone say "wow" or purchase this great ice cream, I needed to develop a profitable way to sell it. This entailed at least a physical location complete with its attendant sales area. Hiring and training personnel would be necessary. I had begun other businesses. I could create this business just as I had done with other businesses in the past. If I followed that path, I would probably get the same result. As long as I was willing to devote almost all of my waking hours to the enterprise, we would have a successful company. We would make a great product and sell enough of that product to be profitable. To the outside world, our company would be a success.

But as I thought more about how I wanted this store to operate, I wanted to go in a different direction. I wanted to have customers saying "wow" time and time again, even if I was absent from the store's daily operations. Even crazier, I might want to have more than this one location. I would want those customers to have the same great experience that they had in our original location. If this goal was to be achieved, I needed to develop a different kind of business model. In this new style of a start-up, I would need to define every facet of the operation. I needed to develop an employee manual, standard operating procedures for all the equipment, checklists for tasks, and so much more. While waiting for a building permit, I ask myself if all of this is necessary to start a simple ice cream shop.

No, it is not. This is the time that I like many entrepreneurs could either lose heart for the entire business, or at least begin to simplify the approach to it. It is more than a bit tempting. It is certainly possible to purchase the necessary equipment to manufacture and market ice cream. No one will keep me from opening my store if I do not have an organizational chart, an employee manual, a mission statement, or standard operating procedures. Almost all small businesses, including all of my past start-ups, do not fret about any of those items. To spend hours writing maintenance notes on various pieces of equipment or detailing how our bathroom should be maintained does not feel like real work compared to developing recipes for an ice cream flavor.

The writing of procedures is work on the actual structure of my business. It is work on operations. It is work on the financials. It is work on marketing. Hopefully, as tiresome as this is, it will be good work for my business. This is an attempt to anchor a dream, a concept, a vision to reality by forcing me to anticipate and articulate for everyone else to see just how we will do things at Cherry Blossom Creamery. Although open to constant revision, this is what Cherry Blossom Creamery will be. The rest is just technical details.

Chapter 10

If you enjoy really good ice cream and revel in an abundance of different flavors, then attending an ice cream trade show is a must-do. As great as the unlimited opportunity to sample ice cream is, it was not the reason I chose to attend the Great Lakes Ice Cream and Fast Foods show in Battle Creek, Michigan.

Attending a trade show is not a new experience for me. When I had my tennis and running store, I was always eager to view what new products and trends were being presented. It was an opportunity to compare and often purchase many of the products that I was going to stock our store. When I had my landscape business, I faithfully walked the mammoth halls looking for a few new varieties of plants or something that would make my company more profitable or ease the workload for my employees. It was with that mindset that I drove to Michigan in February to immerse myself in ice cream and maybe some fast food. I also hoped that a side benefit of this trade show would be the opportunity to meet others who are operating similar enterprises as my own.

It was particularly with this last reason for attending a trade show that I decided to rent a car, pay for a couple of nights' stay at a hotel that I had no other reason for ever staying in, and pay the entrance fee for the show. I had made a list of items I had hoped to find solutions for. Top of the list was packing for our take-away quarts and pints. There were two companies offering the logoed packing I desired. Both required me to purchase and store sizable minimum quantities. Neither seems like a good fit for me. The only item that made my list that I found a good source for was cones. Menu boards, ice cream scoops, free-standing rails, a warmer for melting chocolate, cone displays, and soda dispensers were all absent.

Then, as is the case with all trade shows, I found sources and answers for items I did not know I was even looking for. I found a company that custom makes parts for frozen food machines. He is assembling a one-and-a-half-gallon skirt kit for my dipping case instead of the standard three-gallon skirts. I want to have smaller containers in our dipping cases for many of our flavors. The longer ice cream is allowed to remain where temperatures fluctuate, the less desirable that ice cream becomes. Coffee service is something that I continue to struggle with. It feels like it is a necessity, but I want it to remain simple. I might have found a good resource. Furniture has been in the very back of my mind, but being introduced to an exhibitor at this show, I have become more excited and hope that the quote that he is about to send me will be in the affordable range. The furniture looks great. Finally, I was introduced to a good point-of-sale cash register. There are a lot of extra features, including tracking loyalty rewards, gift cards, pick up ordering, text communication and even employee time clocks. This decision is large enough that I need to do some comparison shopping.

As I was later to discover, most of the vendors that I met at this Midwest show were unable to work with me. I was outside their market area. Although this was ultimately disappointing, the show did help sharpen my list of what I still needed to find if I was to be ready to open in less than a year.

What I did not find was another person that I could talk ice cream business with. I spent an hour at the welcoming breakfast hoping to discover just such a conversation. People talked to me, but everyone there but me seemed to be acquainted with each other. They weren't unwelcoming, but they were at a different place in their ice cream store journey. They did not evince much curiosity in what I was planning and remained uninvolved. In my other businesses that I created, I had always been able to find other business owners who were taking a similar path. Unfortunately, at this show, I did not connect with fellow travelers. I believe it is essential to not just listen to those who are attempting to sell you something or to those who are close to you, but to have the opportunity to refine ideas and share stories with others trying to arrive at a similar destination. Those travelers are out there. I just haven't yet met them.

Chapter 11

Two years is a long time to sit with a concept. It is time enough to question whether your concept is too much or too little. Most businesses are started from a skill set that you possess or from a dissatisfaction with your present employer. There is an organic flow to the process. If you are a great gardener, you might start a landscape business. If you know how to cut hair and are properly licensed, you end up with a hair salon. If you have an accounting degree, you start a financial consulting company. Most businesses are born from past experience or proper accreditation. Because of this easy transition, from the time that the concept is born to its actual realization, a business is up and running rather quickly. It is only then that the absence of proper planning might become apparent.

I had intentionally chosen to begin something that, although I had a strong interest in its product, ice cream, I had no experience in its production or its sale. This truly is a blank sheet of paper and a beginner's mind. This state of mind also allows for trips down other and additional paths from the core concept. I have already pursued making doggie ice cream. I was able to make unique molds so that our doggie ice cream would stand apart. This product will be a part of our store, but I do not believe it to be a strong enough category to devote too much of our efforts to it. Earlier, I had visited a local creperie. I thought long and hard about adding crepes to the ice cream store, but decided it would not quite fit with what I envisioned our store to feel like. Now I am thinking about researching and making snacks. This isn't quite as straightforward as you might imagine.

Do snacks and ice cream make a good combination? Just what are snacks? The category is so huge that there are entire trade shows devoted to their sale. More to the point is, what am I going to consider to be snacks? Snacks can be frozen treats other than ice cream. Snacks can be candy and all candy's permutations. Snacks can be all manner of baked goods. Snacks can be crackers, chips, pretzels, and so many other bagged goodies. Snacks can be so many things. If I am to make snacks a major part of our concept, then I need to define what will classify something as a snack in our store.

To work for us, a snack must be portable. It needs to be able to be bagged or placed in a plastic clamshell container. For us to properly merchandise a snack, it should not need to be frozen or refrigerated. Our snacks should be able to be made in the store or at least be able to be assembled in a unique manner so that they are our snacks. I also believe that unique and wonderful snacks that we are unable to produce and can properly merchandise will be welcome from outside vendors.

If good ice cream is my first love, then tasty snacks come in a close second. I am more than ready to dive into this portion of our business. I have begun compiling recipes for possible snack items. I made black salt and pepper roasted cashews, candied cashews, cinnamon snack mix, Alabama fire crackers, buttery onion pretzels, and spinach balls. I gave samples to my friends and coworkers. The reviews are great. There are a multitude of recipes that I have yet to try.

Is this a good enough idea to actually change the name of our store to Cherry Blossom Creamery and Snack Shop? If we are to produce the snacks in our store, then I need to determine what additional equipment we will need. I know we will need some type of oven or store. What can we use that will not require an exhaust hood or fire suppression? Where can this equipment be placed in our store so that it will be considered a sanitary location? Will we have proper electrical capacity for this new equipment?

I need to look at possible equipment. There is a Restaurant Equipment store in Camp Hill. I need to introduce myself to them and see if they can answer some of my questions.

I am now a member of the Restaurant Store. A fifty-dollar fee entitles Cherry Blossom Creamery to receive special member prices. So far, I have saved about $7.00. I have a ways to go to recap my membership investment. I may not have saved any money yet, but the folks at the store have been friendly, helpful and knowledgeable. I had a few of my questions answered. I now have tamper-evident plastic containers for my snack items. I am still pursuing a label maker, which I will need to finish the snack packaging.

I have also located the convection oven that I believe I desire. It will be going on sale in April. I can wait. Most importantly, the oven will not require a hood or a fire suppression system. I also purchased some cookware that is compatible with my induction oven. With that purchase, I am ready to make some more snacks here in my test kitchen. Many questions remain as to snack production and their marketing, but at least I am making a bit of progress.

Opening a store that makes and sells ice cream is in a stalled position. Once Derry Township decided that I was requesting a zoning change, it opened the handicap accessibility issue. Derry Township will not issue building permits until Labor and Industry approves or gives me a variance to our current handicap accessibility. I need to decide whether to submit a variance application in a normal time frame or to request an expedited hearing for my application. The difference in wait time is enormous. If expedited, I should have my hearing in late April and a decision shortly after. If I submit an application in the regular manner, I will not have a decision for sixty or ninety days. The difference in cost for the two methods of proceeding is significant. To expedite, I need to pay $1440.00 as opposed to $300.00 for the normal application process.

Time is becoming precious. The first day of spring is in the rearview mirror. My mind keeps spiraling through all the challenges that I still have. I do not have a functioning test kitchen. I do not have approved building plans. I do not have a sign permit. I still do not know how to make ice cream, nor where I will sell the ice cream that I hope to someday make. If the obstacles to utilizing the winery space become too huge, I will go back to looking for a location to sell my ice cream. Much as I am experiencing the extremely changing March weather, at one time sunny and warm, and a day later spitting snowflakes, I vacillate from determined and hopeful, to a bit apathetic and defeated. It seems that the only way to move at this time is to pay the extra and expedite my application. At least I will have a better idea of whether my proposed location will be possible.

It was my good fortune that the Labor and Industry inspector who reviewed my expedited application had the good sense to phone me and ask a few questions. He had studied the information that my architect, Chuck, had sent. His question to me was why I was even requesting a variance. It was plain to him that it would be extremely difficult to comply with the accessibility requirement. He indicated that the township should have been able to make that determination and that the twenty per cent requirement should have been invoked. He felt that strongly that he told me that he was going to return my check, as this did not require a hearing.

I thought I now had a path forward for requesting a building permit. I contacted Derry Township and relayed what the Labor and Industry inspector had told me, expecting that would be sufficient. I was informed that the township would require a written note from the inspector before I could move forward. I once again contacted the inspector, and he then forwarded the required note. This episode cost me both time and money. I had to spend money for my architect to take photos and send a narrative to Labor and Industry. I spent time working with both Labor and Industry and the township. It seemed that this question of accessibility should have been straightforward, but somehow I got caught in the slow grinding gears of local government.

Once again, I am thankful that I am not the typical entrepreneur. I certainly want this ice cream business to be successful and profitable, but the ice cream store does not need to be my main source of income.

I also have a very extended period of time to get this business together. If I were more dependent on this venture's income or had to pay the monthly expenses that this delay would be costing me, this enterprise would be in serious difficulty. Almost anyone else starting a business does not have that safety net. It is no wonder that the vast majority of small businesses fail within the first three years.

Chapter 12

Crisis of faith

Spring has come and gone. The first day of summer is no longer a promise, but lies behind me. Cherry Blossom Creamery has made very little progress. My attempt to secure a building permit has stalled. I had gathered all of the paperwork, including the architectural plans and notes from the labor and industry inspector, and submitted them to the township. Three weeks after that submission, I received, instead of an approval, a multi-bullet point comment on the plans. Most of the points I was unable to understand. Other of the points I had thought we had already addressed.

In the meantime, I had taken delivery of several more pieces of equipment and stored them in either my garage or test kitchen. My worry was a combination of having equipment that I was spending more money on and the additional concern that I would never use this equipment. Even worse was the thought that I would be forced to attempt to unload this equipment to someone else. I panicked.

I had sent an email to the plan examiner asking for a face-to-face meeting to discuss the comments that I had received. I wanted my design team and the director of community development also in the meeting. Getting no response for three days made me obsessed with this setback. It was almost five o'clock, and I needed to assume some control. I sent rapid emails to both of the suppliers of my equipment, outlining my problem securing the building permit and indicating that I wanted to put a hold on anymore equipment. I had truly lost faith in this project ever becoming real. I had lost faith in the regulatory system. Most importantly, I had lost faith in my ability to solve the problems that I was encountering. That loss of faith extended to the yet unencountered problems of state licensing, employee recruitment and training, and the nuts and bolts of producing my own ice cream. I was ready to call it a day. I was having a crisis of faith.

Something happened during that evening and throughout a mostly sleepless night. I tried to envision the next four or so years of my life. I realized that all the great things that my life had, a good marriage, great kids and grandkids, the opportunity to travel, and regularly play tennis, still felt lacking. I thought about the effort that I had already expended. I had produced the employee manual, the organizational chart with corresponding job requirements, the logo and outdoor sign design, the layout of the store, the production and growing of the mint for the meadow tea, the creation of unique molds for doggie ice cream, and so much more. I realized that if I were to be truly fulfilled in a creative sense, I either had to continue forward or find something to replace Cherry Blossom Creamery.

At my age, it felt absolutely necessary to have something big and scary in my life. It would be all too easy to retire. I know that if I choose that option, I will be less happy and most likely less healthy. That next morning, when I stopped attempting to sleep, I had achieved clarity. I would go forward with my concept of Cherry Blossom Creamery full speed ahead. I would demonstrate my faith in this project by working at whatever was available to me. I would continue to attempt to arrange the meeting that I needed. I would install the small batch ice cream maker in the test kitchen. I would begin making sample ice cream. I would further refine my business structure. I would find the vendors I needed for my supplies. I would act as if Cherry Blossom Creamery existed. I would act on faith.

Within a week of deciding that I would act as if Cherry Blossom Creamery would come into existence, I was able to schedule a meeting with the plan examiner, the Derry Township director of community development, two of my architects, and myself via Zoom. In what could only be a version of good inspector, bad inspector, the plan examiner prefaced the meeting with a statement that his assistant was very meticulous and strictly by the code. He, having reviewed the permit submission, thought that we could proceed much more simply by declaring a maximum occupancy for the building as twenty-five. As long as Derry Township was ok with this solution instead of having to address several comments that entailed a change of use designation for our building, and most importantly, having to construct a second bathroom, we could proceed with just having to post a sign stating no more than twenty-five in the building. With the meeting going my way, I pushed on two of the other comments. The requirement to show all of the existing electrical circuits was going to cause me a great deal of time and effort. I mentioned that fact and was rewarded with allowing the electrical to be subject to inspection instead of the requirement that I would have had to fulfill. I decided to continue my streak and asked the same question about the plumbing. Here, I was able to not need to detail all of the existing plumbing, but I did need to note where the floor drains were going to feed into the main drain for the building. Then the inspector added a note. He wanted a study of the weight-bearing limits for the floor in the building.

As usual, each step of this process required more work for me. The meeting went very well, but I still had to satisfy the plumbing and weight-bearing questions. On the way back from the meeting, I phoned my plumber and discussed the information we needed. He had questions that I was most unable to answer, so I got the architect, Rob, to phone the plumber, Henry, and get the information that they needed. Once home, I took a tape measure, a clipboard, and a flashlight to the crawl space under the building. I measured and sketched the beam and its supporting towers. I measured the cross joints. With the new information in hand, I phoned Rob. Hopefully, we are full speed ahead.

The devil in the details rose once again. We had to change the use designation of our proposed location from a M for merchantile to a B for business because we were producing the ice cream on site. We now fall under the present building code and not the one that the winery had existed under. One of the changes entailed the weight requirements for what the floor needed to support. It now had to conform to one hundred pounds per square foot and not the fifty pounds per square foot that had been the case. A revised plan needed to be produced by the architect, noting the extra pillars and extra support beam, which was then forwarded to the plan examiner. His approval followed. An estimate of nearly eleven thousand dollars from a contractor to rectify this situation also followed, causing me once again to question the wisdom of continuing. I decided that the B classification was a major improvement to the value of this property, and since I was the owner of said property, it made sense to move forward.

Two pieces of equipment arrived. My small batch freezer from Carpigiana and my pasteurizer were installed. I contacted my ice cream mix supplier, Valley Farms Dairy, and they were kind enough to supply some samples. I then placed an order from my seminar friend, Malcolm, for cocoa, coconut milk, vanilla, stabilizer and other items that I would need. I shopped locally for frozen strawberries, mangoes, sugar, and other ingredients from the recipes that I would first attempt.

I did my best to follow the recipes, and I was amazed at the ice cream that I was producing right from the start. I used only the best ingredients. I did my best to properly clean and sanitize my equipment. I now understand why the base for the dairy-free ice cream needed to be pasteurized. It had nothing to do with food safety. What it accomplished was to take a lumpy mix of ingredients and turn it into a smooth milk-like substance that allowed for a creaminess in the dairy-free flavors that no other method could duplicate.

As I produced more and more flavors of ice cream, I began to give them to many of my friends as well as my neighbors in my commercial building. There were no bad reviews. Of course, when you are getting free ice cream, you probably will not be too critical. I did receive some glowing reviews, which I thought were hopefully heartfelt.

I continued to learn about my small batch ice cream maker as I tried new recipes. I was unable to include larger pieces of fruit or pieces of nuts or candy, or cake into the mix as it was forming an ice cream. If I wanted any of these items in the finished product, I had to mix them in as I was extruding the ice cream. This was not ideal. I was assured that the larger batch freezer, which would be my workhorse once we were in the production room at our actual location, would not have this problem. In the meantime, I was making flavors that did not require many or any inclusions.

Chapter 13

Making ice cream was very satisfying. Having other people tell you how good it tasted was even more satisfying. All that good feeling distracted me from the work that still needed to be done if this ice cream shop was ever going to open. The summer had quickly fled, and it was the beginning of October. It was only two months from taking possession of the property and only three months from the anticipated installation of the equipment. Before that could happen, we needed to find a project that would allow us to spend the required twenty percent of the renovation costs so that we would be in compliance with Labor and Industry standards. We had to reinforce the floor to meet the new code requirements. We then needed to build the new walls for the production room. We needed to cover the walls in the production room with FRP to be more sanitary. The other walls needed to be painted. New flooring in the production room and the sitting area needed to be installed. Appropriate plumbing and electrical systems needed to be installed.

Once some or all of these tasks were accomplished, there were inspections from the code enforcement officer that needed to be scheduled and hopefully passed. There was also the need to somehow obtain the necessary licenses, which included a frozen dessert license, a milk license, and a restaurant license from the Commonwealth of Pennsylvania. It is daunting.

In mid-September, Sue and I had taken a two-week trip to several national parks in Montana, Oregon, and Washington. There were a few moments from that trip that helped to inspire me to continue my quest for my ice cream store. In eastern Oregon, we stumbled upon a town called Hot Springs. This town was twenty-five miles from the nearest larger town. It had used effective signage along the highway advertising what businesses that existed in Hot Springs. Signs were placed every quarter mile reminding me on a much smaller scale of how South of the Border advertises as you are driving along 1-95. With little else to see, it built momentum, causing you to think about stopping. Tired of driving, we decided to take a right turn and visit Hot Springs. This was a town that was really trying. There were quite a few small businesses that had a well-kept appearance and were definitely open for business. We eventually found the organic food store, complete with a bakery that we had seen advertised. Once inside, we were impressed. The bakery items were plentiful and looked delicious. The couple of items we tasted certainly were mouth-watering good. I asked the person serving us just how big this town was. She replied that it had six hundred residents. I could only marvel at the investment in equipment and time that this bakery had required. I could only applaud their effort and enthusiasm. I could only reflect that if this bakery in the smallest of towns in the middle of nowhere could succeed, then Cherry Blossom Creamery had an excellent chance of succeeding as well. Just the fact of this little bakery existing was enough to place in perspective my difficulties that lay ahead, although formidable, were probably less difficult than what this bakery had successfully navigated.

It is not that easy to find a project that fulfills the requirement of increased accessibility and yet is the correct financial size to be feasible. I originally wanted to increase the width of the sidewalk connecting the rear parking lot to the back door, but was informed that should I attempted this, then the entire sidewalk would have to conform to current code requirements. This sidewalk is far too steep for that to occur unless we built a sidewalk with multiple switchbacks. The cost for this would exceed what we were spending on the entire renovation. We could make improvements in the bathroom and possibly the two steps separating the upper and lower levels, but these would not cost enough to fulfill the twenty percent requirements. Finally, we decided that we would make the handicap parking space in the rear parking lot truly handicap accessible. It needed to have a slope of less than two percent. This would require considerable expense.

It was October, and the handicap parking space was finally getting built. My carpenter installed the extra courses of retaining wall. The paving contractor brought back fill and paved the space. All that is left is for the line painter to properly mark the space. When that is finished, I can call for my first of many inspections and hopefully take this troublesome item off my list.

The long-awaited handicap parking space is finished. The call has been made, and I await this critical inspection. The paving contractor assured me that he has accomplished the necessary under a two percent grade. The line painter assures me that we will be in proper compliance. But if what I did to satisfy the accessibility issue is not approved, I don't know how we are going to fix it. It was mid-November, and the weather would be anything but cooperative depending on what we might be required to do. If Cherry Blossom Creamery is to open on my now hoped-for date of March 3, 2023, this portion of the project must be approved in a few days. The inspection is scheduled in three days.

I could not merely wait for the accessibility inspection; I have so many different tasks that need to be accomplished, so it was time to continue down my list. Permitting was next. It has been an onerous task, but I have finally completed the applications for the food establishment license and the frozen desserts license. The applications included a scaled drawing of the placement of all the equipment. The equipment needed to be numbered and listed according to use, manufacturer, and model number. The treatment for the walls, ceilings, lighting, and floors needed to be detailed for all portions of the ice cream store. Information concerning Cherry Blossom Creamery's ownership was required. Proof of Pennsylvania sales tax license and the completion of a Safe Serv course needed to be included. After copies were made of all pertinent pages, the applications were on their way to the Pennsylvania Department of Agriculture. Hopefully, in four to six weeks, I will be interacting with their food inspectors.

Reviewing the three-pronged approach that I had taken to begin this venture, I am mostly positive about where I now stand. I have a building permit, even though it requires extra steps that are costing me more time and much more money. I have spent enough time with my smaller ice cream equipment to confidently produce excellent ice cream. The new, larger equipment will present another learning curve. I am confident that the extra cost of setting up the test kitchen will be an excellent investment in helping me master the new equipment. Lastly, the applications for licensing are on their way, even though I am sure I will need to make some modifications for them to be approved. So what now?

The build-out of the store needs to be scheduled. The first step is the opening of the present floor so that the beams and supports underneath that floor can be adequately reinforced. The new wall that will enclose the production area has to be constructed, complete with a glass door so that customers can actually view the production of the ice cream they are about to eat. The new subfloor must then be installed. Walls need to be painted. New floor covering needs to be installed. The storage areas will need shelves to be installed. All of this needs to be accomplished before the thirteen pieces of ice cream production and sales equipment need to be delivered and then installed.

Parallel to all of this is the purchasing of the chairs and tables, both to be used for inside and outside dining. All the paper supplies, including take-out containers, serving cups, coffee cups, and on and on, need to be sourced, ordered, and delivered. The test kitchen has forced me to find some of the sources for the ice cream ingredients, but many more items will be necessary and often in more economical sizes than what I am currently familiar with. I must decide on the uniforms that will be our signature look. The computer system, complete with payment options, must be purchased. What phone system will I use? There are still systems that need to be created. The organizational chart is not finished, which means that some of the job descriptions are not written. With time to think and having spoken with other ice cream shop operators, there are several additions that need to be made to the employee manual. I am overwhelmed but also excited about what it is I am creating. Now I am waiting for the accessibility inspection.

Chapter 14

Battle of the levels

As badly as I feared the accessibility inspection might go, it went even worse. Immediately upon exiting his vehicle, the township inspector informed me that the handicap space had to be van accessible and not car accessible. He showed me that on our drawings, there was noted both a van and a car accessible spot. Although both were noted, the code required the van option. This would require an additional three feet of less than two percent grading. It would require new paving, a new retaining wall, and new line striping. He then placed his electronic level on our parking space and announced that it exceeded the required maximum slope. I was dumbfounded. I felt that my architect had let me down by not understanding the need for the van space. I felt my paving contractor had not done the job he had been contracted to do. I could see the architect and the paver blaming each other. Either way, the financial hardship was going to fall on me. The suggestion that the inspector made that I felt most likely to go with was to request a variance once again from Labor and Industry. Spending the extra money to get where he told me I needed to go was a big ask.

After spending my day immersed in a funk, at ten minutes to five, I got a phone call from my township inspector with regard to our accessibility compliance. He said he had discussed this problem with the township director of community development and that they had decided that if Labor and Industry had approved a handicap space that led to a non compliant side walk which led to a non compliant back entrance, then they felt comfortable making this handicap space car and not van accessible. This was a huge victory as I now had to only address the slope issue.

I phoned my paving contractor and he and I set up a time to meet at the site. He arrived with a new electronic level and proceeded to take spot measurements, determining the slope both north and south and east and west. All but one reading on his level was below two percent. The one outlier was at two point two percent. Now I was caught between my paver telling me we were in compliance and the inspector telling me we were outside of that compliance. My paving contractor requested that he and the inspector meet and discuss this discrepancy. The meeting was arranged. My paving contractor was to arrive with his new level. The inspector was to arrive with his level, and he informed me that he was bringing a second level. I would be there to witness this duel of the levels, and Sue, my wife, would be there to photograph the different readings.

The duel was set for 4:30 on Thursday. The participants arrived: Mick from code enforcement, Joe from the paving company, I as a witness, and my wife, Sue, as the photographer. Mick brought two levels that he assured us had just been recalibrated. Joe only had his brand-new level. The readings did not match. Mick consistently got readings of greater than 2.5 per cent in certain areas of the parking space. Joe's level never got reading above two percent at the same spots. Sue photographed all the readings. Finally, Mick stated that he had no idea why Joe was getting different readings, but he suspected that Joe's level was incorrectly calibrated. Regardless, Mick decided to accept Joe's level. Joe quickly picked up his level and left. I walked briskly to the outdoor box where the plans and the inspection cards were kept and brought the inspection card to Mick. Mick signed beside the accessibility inspection line. One hurdle crossed.

But it seems there are always new and unexpected hurdles. The same day that we got past the accessibility issue, I received a call from the company that is doing my outdoor sign informing me that they had encountered difficulties in obtaining the needed sign permit from Derry Township. They explained to me that the sign I was requesting would need a variance from the township. According to their sign ordinance, only one directional sign was allowed per property. They also indicated that the sign had to be ground level, when in fact the sign I was proposing to replace was four feet off the ground. I had visited both of these concerns before and received a variance, which is why the sign that currently occupies the space I was requesting was in fact a free-standing sign four feet off the ground. I phoned the sign ordinance enforcement officer in the hopes that this issue could be resolved quickly and without additional expense to me.

That was not going to be the case. Once again, the logic was that because we were changing the status of the building from a Class M to a Class B, we now had to come into compliance with the current building code. I would need to complete an application for a sign variance asking for permission to have my free-standing sign, and that it be not at ground level, but four feet above the ground. I would need to present my case at a zoning variance board meeting. Of course, there were more fees. I was assured that there was a very good chance that my variance would be granted, but by this point in this project, I am tired of fighting. I want to work on the business of Cherry Blossom Creamery, and I need to know all the prerequisites necessary to open this store. I had an out. If I merely changed the existing painted wooden sign that was advertising the winery with a new painted wooden sign that was advertising Cherry Blossom Creamery, I did not need to obtain any additional approvals. The outdoor sign that I would be getting was not exactly what I desired, but it would allow me to move on. I did check with the sign company I was using, and they assured me that they could modernize the lighting with LED lights, which would match the light output of the interior illuminated sign that I had first ordered. If they are correct about the lighting, then I saved myself not just time and frustration, but also a significant amount of money. With each day, there seems to be either another unexpected expense or an expense that is larger than had been planned. Saving any money felt so good.

As our hoped-for store opening is only three months away, more and more decisions have to be made. The existing carpet in the seating area and production room, although great looking, is not appropriate for an ice cream store. After visiting the store, my flooring contractor and I decided that luxury vinyl would be suitable. He left a sample book, but before I had even studied the samples, he phoned. There was a close-out style available, but I had to act immediately. The picture looks good. I told him to lock that style in. He did, and I thought that I could check off another task from my list and that I had gotten a bargain. It is never that easy.

In order to reinforce the floor of my new store to meet current code, we have to add a support beam and build several columns. All of this takes place in the crawl space under the store. The space at the front end is open enough for me to stand in, but as it goes to the rear of the building, the opening decreases to where it is only a foot or so. To build the necessary supports in such a tight space is going to be problematic. Since we are replacing the floor covering above the crawl space that is the tightest, it makes sense to cut openings in the existing floor. Once the reinforcing is complete, the subfloor will be closed, and the flooring will be ready for my chosen luxury vinyl. It also seemed like a good idea to inform the plumber of this opening in the floor. I hoped that this might make his job easier when he was connecting to existing pipes or installing grease traps. We met, and it was going to make his job easier.

If I followed his advice, my life was going to get harder. He was not keen on the luxury vinyl planking in the production room due to the amount of water that is likely to find its way onto the flooring during the making of the ice cream. Nor was he happy about how the floor drain would tie into the luxury vinyl. He strongly suggested either ceramic tile, a poured floor, or at least a single sheet of vinyl be our chosen floor. I knew that Dan, my flooring guy, had ordered this luxury vinyl style only for me, and that this style was being discontinued. In all likelihood, Dan was not going to be thrilled with my new request. Much as I hated thinking that I was wasting money, it made sense to correct the error now. If I made a mistake in the choice of material, it made no sense to continue on that path, even if it meant paying for and not using a portion of the material that Dan had purchased for me.

An additional discussion with Dan, my flooring guy, and quite possibly fatigue on my part, has convinced me to remain with the luxury vinyl flooring in the production room. Dan had done many installations where there was some water involved on the flooring and assured me that I had little to fret about. I did agree with Mike, the plumber, that we needed a larger floor drain. This would allow less spillage when pouring our bucket while cleaning the batch freezer. Of course, there is an additional charge.

Chapter 15

The pace of this project has at times felt glacial. Not today. It is day four of having the rental space to myself. I had spent a portion of the weekend marking the layout of the equipment. It is extremely difficult to look at a piece of paper and sense the visual layout or the flow of the store. I used masking tape to mark where the equipment would go on the downstairs hardwood floors. That floor, I would be retaining. In the upstairs where the carpet was not going to remain, I used spray paint to mark that equipment. Even this was not making me feel comfortable. I decided to construct with paper the sizes of some of the equipment. I could easily move these paper models around to determine if this layout would work. A second reason for this obsessive behavior stemmed from a meeting that I had had with Tim, my refrigeration equipment person.

Tim and I met on day one of having this space to myself. We wanted to confirm our ability to move several of the large pieces of equipment through the existing door openings. We found problems. The reach-in freezer and reach-in refrigerator were not going to fit through the back door. Good alternatives are in short supply. The best we could come up with was to wheel them from the back parking lot all the way around the side of the building and then through the large front doors. That would, if everything went right, get them into the building. From our permit plans, both pieces of equipment had to be installed on the upper level. They had to travel up the three steps that separated the downstairs level from the upper level. If we are able to realize that goal, then the refrigerator would find its way to the back of the production room with little difficulty. Not so for the freezer. It needed to go through two doors and a hallway that were not large enough to allow it to reach its final destination without rebuilding doors or walls. It was because of this development that I needed to find an alternative spot for the freezer.

With the help of my paper cutouts, I found space in the downstairs area. Technically, I should have requested a building permit adjustment. This would entail a new sealed drawing from my architect, four copies of that new drawing, and the permit adjustment application to the township. This entire process would result in additional charges, but even more importantly, possible delays. My plumber felt that there was a different solution to this problem. He suggested that I place the freezer in the location that I had now chosen and that I plead ignorance and explain that it was impossible to place this piece of equipment where it was designated on the existing drawing.

After considerable hesitation, I agree with Mike. There is one other problem with this decision. This freezer weighs all but eight hundred pounds and will be placed on a portion of the floor that is not being reinforced as per the building plans. The company doing the floor reinforcement, COR, determined that it would be a good idea to do some modest reinforcement because of this additional weight. Initially, I agreed. Waking in the middle of the night, which has become an all too common occurrence of late, I revisited that decision. I realized that if we reinforced that area, it would be extremely difficult to hide the fact that we knew that this new location was where the freezer was always bound for. If, during inspection, it was determined we needed to add the reinforcement, we could do so. Even if we are not required to do this additional reinforcement, I will have it done once we obtain our occupancy permit.

The pace of the project continues to accelerate. Mike, the plumber, is about to reroute the sewer connection and move some plumbing that is in the way of the reinforcing columns that need to be built. He has ordered the grease traps, faucets for the sinks, and is helping me determine how to lay out the soda dispensing unit.

With the accelerated pace has come a basketful of questions. The carpenters need to know where to frame out the floor sink for the grease trap. This is a bigger decision and one that I had given no prior thought to. Do I want to have to stand on the plastic cover when I am using the batch freezers, or would it be better if I were standing on this plastic grate while working at the prep table? I really would not like to stand on it at all. Now we are thinking that putting the drain in front of the hardening cabinet will be the least bothersome for the staff while we are making ice cream. I also have to think about what our customers will see when they look through the glass door into our production room. After consultations with our plumbing crew and our carpenter crew, we think we can by placing the drain directly in front of the hardening cabinet block the view from our glass door enough that our customers will not be witnessing our workers dumping the wastewater into the drain. We want our customers to see the magic of ice cream production without the attendant clean-up activities.

What color is the store going to be? Until recently, I had the luxury of sitting with a question for days, maybe months. What would my logo look like? What equipment did I need to produce and serve the ice cream? What is the store concept? Now decisions are needed. They are needed quickly without that foregone luxury of time. My brother-in-law is undertaking the painting of the inside of the store. He needs to know what color is going where. I wish to be somewhat consistent with the colors that we have chosen for our logo in our outdoor sign. I have picked out a pink color and a blue color that mimic those sign colors. I don't want the entire store to be this two-color combination, so I have chosen a sand beige color for a few walls in the front area. I am going to use this sand color in all the storage and employee areas that our customers will not see. I thought I was done with the colors, but I was wrong. The bathroom is very dull, so I chose a lighter blue to bring it to life. Then I was asked what I wanted to do with the window trims and baseboards. At this point, I would just like them freshly painted and in a color that did not require a decision. I know I need to work on this question, and I will. I just need a few minutes without a question.

It is Friday, just one week since this space has been entirely mine, and there has been a lot of progress. The inspector signed off on the footer depth and placement for the floor reinforcement. This allowed the carpenter crew to continue onto their next step, which was to pour the concrete for these footers. They will return on Monday and install the support beams. While this was taking place, I had the opportunity to meet with my electrician. We reviewed where all the equipment would be placed and what he needed to provide to properly power that equipment. As is most often the case, he made me aware of something that I had not thought about. We will need power to the dipping cases and to our point of sale area. More electrical circuits, more additional cost to the original estimate.

It is odd, but there seems to be, by the way all the subcontractors are scheduling, that an unspoken agreement has been reached that it is our goal to be finished with the build-out by the end of the year. This is not a date that I thought had any chance of being achieved. If this is possible, I am extremely excited. The equipment is going to be shipped on January 2. If we can reach this end-of-year goal, it would be amazing. Having the equipment moved in by early January would allow me to leave for our planned vacation with a much lighter heart. Sue and I have booked our two-week trip to Key West with a departure date of January 16. I always thought that we would be moving equipment after we returned. If we could have this done prior to that vacation, I could be a lot more relaxed while eating dinner outside at Santiago Bogeda and hopefully, better company for Sue.

Chapter 16

I had wanted something in my life to give it a purpose. I wanted something that would make me be alert. I wanted a new venture that asked me new questions and forced me to learn new things. I wanted to attempt to create a business unlike any I had operated before. I wanted to build a self-sufficient, vibrant, useful business. All of that, I hope, is occurring with Cherry Blossom Creamery. Sometimes I need to disengage. What has been an effective vehicle for that disengagement has been the large, almost monumental, stain glass mosaic project.

One of my tenants had suggested that a friend of hers would paint a mural on the side of our commercial building. She thought that this would generate visits, as it was a trending item to have a selfie taken in front of murals in different locales. I considered the idea and thought it had merit. This discussion occurred just before the pandemic. Like every other business, she and her consignment store took a pause. Murals took a back seat to somehow remaining open and generating revenue. I, on the other hand, had abundant time to explore this mural idea. I learned that if we were to go forward with painting a mural, I would need to get a permit from the township.

The more I pondered this, the more I had no desire to involve the township, but what I did like was the idea of doing a collection of stain glass panels instead of painting a mural. If we proceeded in this manner, I would envision the panels being hung after winter was over and removed before winter returned. This would classify the endeavor as an artistic installation. No need for a permit. I decided that nine two-foot by two-foot panels arranged three across would provide a backdrop for selfies and make the building that much more interesting. The subject matter became apparent while driving around Hershey in mid-spring. The weeping cherries are so striking that it was an easy choice to try and depict them. The grass around the bottom of the cherry tree would display spring flowers such as daffodils. Tulips, crocuses, and snowdrops. A few animals, such as a squirrel or a rabbit or a couple of flying birds, would complete the artwork. To proceed, all that was needed was an original design that could accommodate stain glass and the endless hours to build each of the nine panels. A very important side benefit to this concept was the name of our ice cream store. Looking at the design, the name of our store, Cherry Blossom Creamery, became apparent. It seemed to evince happiness, springtime hope, and an endeavor worth pursuing.

Having a name for our store that I really liked was great. All that needed to be accomplished now was the building of the nine panels. Each was taking on average two months to complete. That is a long time, but I am a part-time stain glass worker. Truth be told, I am not fast, nor do I think very skilled. Both of those qualities lead to a slow build-out. The deficiencies I often display in this craft are more than made up for by the absolute beauty of the stain glass.

Break over. It is time to wrestle with a problem in our layout of the store. The back-to-back dipping cases, when marked off on the floor, take up more room than they appear to on the architectural drawing. What I am left with is an area that is very small for the point of sale, our checkout area. As small as that area is, the aisle into the area behind the point of sale is even more troublesome. I want a larger checkout area and a significantly larger aisle into the area behind the dipping cases. I have wrestled with this problem, and I decided to contact our equipment supplier and attempt to cancel our twelve-can unit and replace it with an eight-can unit. If we can do this, we can build a larger checkout area and allow for much better access to the working area.

My e-mail to Tim generated an immediate response. He contacted Global, which is the manufacturer of the dipping cases, and was informed that it would be ten to twelve weeks before we would receive the requested eight-can unit. If we remain with our initial order, we would see shipment in early January, just three weeks away. With a wish for the opening of March 3, waiting for the desired eight-unit can was very unattractive. There has to be a way to accomplish the two needs of more checkout space and better accessibility. Those paper models of my equipment are once again in use. I have moved one of the cases to the front wall and placed the other case perpendicular to it. I need to sit with this possible solution for a bit. If we go with this, the floor drain will need to be moved as well.

Before making this drastic change in equipment layout, I decided to contact Mick, the township code enforcement officer whom I had worked with. My question to him was: Can I move the cabinets without having to submit new drawings and request a permit modification? The second question was: Can I not build the small knee wall that was in the plans? This wall served little purpose other than to give the electrician a spot to install his outlets for the dipping cases. Of course, the information that Mick supplied was not what I expected. He was willing to eliminate the knee wall without the need for permit modification, but he reminded me that the checkout counter had to be handicap accessible. I was not aware of this regulation. It required at least four feet of entry parallel to the checkout counter, which would allow access for a wheelchair. The checkout counter also had to be no more than 36" high. The new information made the decision as to the location of the dipping cabinets much easier. They needed to stay one against the other as they appeared in the sealed drawing. The floor drain could remain as it was. The point of sale counter needed to be in line with the cabinets, and all of us would have to deal with the smaller-than-desired opening to the area behind the dipping cabinets.

This was not the only compromise that I made this week. While working in my test kitchen for the last months, I had become concerned about the milk waste that is flushed from the batch freezer when the batch freezer is cleaned between flavors or at the end of the production day. In the test kitchen, I poured the worst of this into a five-gallon bucket and eventually threw the liquid in this bucket out in the grass beside my back door. Throwing a portion of a five-gallon bucket out every two or three days, while not ideal, still worked. This was not a good plan for the amount of production that we would soon be undertaking. I thought a grease flow collector would be a good idea. An idea good enough to include in the production room, even though it had not been required, nor was it on our drawings. An idea good enough to order this piece of equipment. When it arrived, I was surprised by its size and weight. My plumber explained that there would always be water in the bottom of the trap, and the grease, in this case, fats, would separate and be on the surface of this rather large basin. Periodically, it would be necessary to open the lid and skim the fat layer and pour this layer into a bucket. The thick liquid in the bucket now needed to be properly disposed of. One of the plumbers commented that there was often a strong and offensive odor that accompanied the cleaning of the grease collector. This is not what I was hoping for. I decided that the plumbers needed to better understand what would be going down the drain that led directly to the sewer. I did not want the milk waste to cause blockages in my wastewater lines.

Before the plumbers arrived in the morning, I got an early start and made a small batch of vanilla ice cream. I followed that with a small batch of dulce de Leche. I collected the milk waste between flavors and at the end of the production. I had about half of a five-gallon bucket. The plumbers poured a bit of this liquid into a small bucket and left it sit for a few minutes. They also emptied the five-gallon bucket into the grass. They then examined the liquid in the small bucket and saw very little separation of the fat. It was their opinion that I did not need the grease interceptor. My happiness from not needing to install this unwieldy piece of equipment was tempered by the fact that I was stuck with this same unwieldy piece of equipment. The plumber could not take it back. This is a costly error.

Another compromise was just around the corner. The hardwood floors in the serving area were quite attractive, but in need of sanding and refinishing. I thought I had found the right person for this job, but several attempts to contact him failed. Not being able to contact him was a hurdle, but a larger hurdle was that once the refinishing was completed, it would require at least a week during which we needed to not be on the newly refinished floors, not allowing us to work in that area. With the delivery of our large equipment looming ever closer, we could not afford to lose that much time. A call to my flooring guy, Dan, resulted in an additional order of luxury vinyl. The hardwood floor would be replaced with a new, and ultimately less attractive choice. Time is not waiting for anyone.

In other areas of the construction, we had made excellent time. The plumbers had gotten all of the rough plumbing done. They had even removed the very old cast iron sewer pipe and replaced it with PVC pipe. The electrician was well on his way to finishing the rough electrical connections. The carpenters had built their wall and helped install floor drains where necessary. They even suggested that they would replace the existing drop ceiling in the production room with vinyl-clad tiles. These would be more sanitary and easier to keep clean. They would do this for only the cost of the materials and not charge for the labor to install them. Although not required, this would make for a great look in the production room.

It was time to call Derry Township and request the next two inspections. The rough plumbing and rough frame out inspections passed with only one comment. It is always the one comment that will cost additional money. Mick, our inspector, wrote that there needed to be some type of heater installed in the crawl space below the store to ensure that the water lines would not freeze. This is not on the plans nor in the budget. The upcoming freakishly cold temperatures forecast in the next few days only add urgency to this requirement.

The predicted low temperatures arrived. In fact, the thermometer recorded a low of two degrees, three degrees lower than called for. I had slept poorly on Thursday, worrying about how this freezing weather would affect the newly installed plumbing in the crawl space. It was with much relief that Ken, my electrician, returned on Friday, installing the heater just as the temperature was doing its rapid descent. He also finished the rough electrical work in preparation for the electrical inspection on Tuesday. My brother-in-law, Rich, continues to do more than I expect. He has almost finished all of the painting. The blue and pink combination in the serving area sure makes for an upbeat feel. If we pass the electrical inspection, we will probably be ready for the shipment of ice cream equipment. Reaching that goal seemed quite improbable when we took possession of the store on December 1.

The electrical inspection did not go quite like I had hoped. The inspector made a note. It is always the note. The note indicated that because this is a commercial building, the wire that was run both below the floor and the wire that was run above the drop ceiling needed additional protection. My electrician, Ken, promised that he would speak with the inspector and determine what he would need to do in order to have our project pass inspection. The good portion of the inspection was that the inspector signed off on this first inspection. This allows our workers to close the walls and continue the build-out of our shop.

Just a note of my own. It seems odd that the manner in which Ken ran the wire in this commercial application was not correct, but if it had been a residential job, the inspector would have been fine with the method of wiring. Do homes have less chance of catching on fire? Then the other curious item. There is a fair amount of wiring that was done to this property that we are not modifying. The overhead lights, the exhaust fans, and many of the outlets are examples. I quizzed the inspector about the old wiring and whether we would have to redo it. His response was that we only needed to be concerned with the new wiring. If the wiring that pre-existed our build-out is ok, then why are we worried about the new wiring? Like I said, is it just my note?

The construction has been my main focus for the last three weeks, but there are a lot more things that need to be accomplished if we are going to make a March opening. I made a list that included building a website, selecting uniforms, finding furniture, ordering paper supplies, obtaining a phone number, and choosing payment options for our customers. My daughter, Meghan, had asked what I wanted for Christmas. I requested that she spend a few hours with me working on some of the many computer-related issues. We had our first two hours together. She helped me open a Google account, obtain a Google email address and purchase our domain and hosting service. Not all has gone smoothly as the domain site doesn't seem to recognize our attempts at securing the name, Cherry Blossom Creamery. I have forwarded all appropriate emails to my web designer, Jonathan. I am confident he will get us to our goal. I am also confident that Meghan now wishes she had bought me a nice gift instead of offering her assistance. I need to tell her that it is one of the best gifts that anyone has given me.

No surprise to me, Jonathan was able to work past the verification problems with our web hosting company. We have the domain name of Cherry Blossom Creamery, and Jon is beginning the build-out of our website. I have contracted Comcast for our internet service and for them to supply our landline. Soon we will have a phone number.

A phone number and a website address allow me to work on other items necessary to be completed before our opening. Next items include ordering office supplies that include business cards, stationery, and envelopes. It is time to order our take-out containers and the logo stickers that will be affixed to them. I needed either a phone number or a web address to allow our customers a way to get back in touch after they try our handmade ice cream.

The pace has been quick. In just thirty days, we reinforced the floor, did all of the rough plumbing, did all of the rough electrical, built the production room, painted the majority of the store, and installed new flooring. During that time, we had to pass accessibility, footer, rough electric, rough plumbing, and rough framing. We are now ready for the equipment to arrive and be moved into place.

The date of the equipment's arrival could be problematic. Sue and I scheduled our two-week trip to Key West months ago. It is very likely that thirteen very heavy and difficult-to-maneuver pieces of equipment will arrive during a time that I will not be available. My brother-in-law, Rich, has stepped forward to be there to supervise and help with the move-in. I am trying to do everything I can to provide Rich with enough information to make this move-in go correctly. I have placed tape on the floor outlining the placement of each piece of equipment. In the area inside these marked areas, I have taped a piece of paper with the name, model number, identifying number from the permit drawings, and dimensions of that particular piece of equipment. I will meet with Rich, go over the plan, and hope that I have prepared sufficiently that everything will be in the location I desire when I return.

Now that all of the walls have been built and the flooring installed, the act of laying out all of the equipment has allowed me to possibly modify the placement of a few pieces of equipment. Another meeting with the plumbers is in order. That meeting will take place on Wednesday. I want to see if we can place the pasteurizer beside the batch freezers. If we are able to do this, we will be able to eliminate the additional sink. That sink will crowd the area around the three-bay sink. Another sink is not aesthetically pleasing and hopefully not needed.

Just received a call from Richard Love that he is ready to bring and hopefully install his two pieces of equipment. He will be bringing the larger batch freezer and the soft serve machine on Thursday. Tim, from Commercial Refrigeration, has scheduled the smaller worktop refrigeration to be delivered on the following Tuesday. While his crew is here, they will move the small batch freezer and larger worktop refrigeration unit from the test kitchen to our store. Before we return from Key West, my test kitchen will be disassembled. I snapped a few pictures. Although it was an extra expense, I believe that having the ability to work on ice cream flavor recipes and finding where to secure the needed ingredients for those recipes will have been worth that expense.

The timing for so many things has become compressed. Partly it is the momentum that has been generated by all the people working on this project, and partly because Sue and I are leaving town for two weeks. There are many wheels turning, but it continues to be very difficult to complete any task. All last week, I worked on four different projects without completing any of them. I worked with our screen printer and embroidery team in an effort to finalize store uniforms and t-shirt merchandise. We haven't yet come upon the right tag line to go with the large logo on the t-shirts. We have not settled on the color for the staff shirt, nor given final approval to the artwork.

I met with the packaging company that I hope will do our ice cream tubs and our take-out containers. I was unable to decide whether we would use plastic or cardboard. Once again, I do not have a decision on the tag line. I await pricing, but that will not be the deciding factor. I just need to determine what will be best for Cherry Blossom Creamery.

I have to decide on a point of sale system.

What I thought would be the easiest task to complete became the largest time-waster of all. I wanted to contract with Comcast to provide my phone and internet service. After agreeing to the terms and price for the contract, Comcast informed me that they do not have service at my address. When Cullari had the winery, his address was the same as the other larger building on this property, namely, 1251 E. Chocolate Ave. I requested that my store have a different address, and Derry Township allowed that my address would be 1241 E. Chocolate Ave. Comcast could not authenticate my new address. The customer sales rep asked me for something official that had Cherry Blossom Creamery and the new address on it. My permit had the combined address. My EIN number certificate had my home address, as we obtained that EIN number almost two years ago. I scrambled about and finally found some invoices that had been made out to Cherry Blossom Creamery and had the correct address on them. I took pictures of these invoices and forwarded those pictures to Greta at Comcast. A day later, she informed me that this was not sufficient to authenticate my address. My next step was to drive to Derry Township's office and explain my dilemma. After looking into the situation, Chuck, the community development officer, suggested that a letter needed to be drafted and sent to the post office, the tax office and to me confirming the change of address. This process took another day. I then emailed this letter to Greta. Another day passed before this letter was ultimately accepted. A new contract needed to be sent, and the document signed. Eight days and way too much time had been spent accomplishing this very straightforward task. I could only speculate what Comcast thought I wanted with an address that they could not verify.

They viewed Google Maps and saw that my new address was less than seventy feet from the old address. An address that they serviced. This chapter is not yet over, as Comcast needs to do a site survey to see how expensive or possible it will be for them to provide the service I requested.

Chapter 17

It is time for a break. A break, whether or not I desire it. The date for our annual two-week vacation to Key West has arrived. When I chose this time for our vacation many months ago, I tried to anticipate just how close I would be to having Cherry Blossom Creamery up and running. I thought that the last two weeks of January would be a time when not much would be occurring. I hoped that these two weeks would be used to finish a lot of the electrical, plumbing, and construction. I guessed incorrectly. The initial build-out occurred more quickly than I had hoped for. The remainder of the large equipment was shipped sooner than I had been led to believe would happen. What I feared most was about to come to pass. Several very heavy pieces of ice cream equipment will be delivered and hopefully installed while Sue and I are in Key West. Not ideal. Fortunately, I have a great brother-in-law who will be there to make sure everything happens without a hitch.

That is what I tell myself as I walk in the early morning around beautiful Key West. Every time I return to Key West, I am struck anew by its beautiful architecture, its flowering trees, and its lush vegetation. Key West doesn't so much change, but my reaction to Key West often changes. Since 1972, I have been spending anywhere from a few days to several weeks in this tropical paradise. There have been several years that I have missed this trip, but I have gone often enough to realize how much I have changed over the past five decades. My first time there, I could feel the energy and the rawness of the town. I sensed the potential. When I returned to Hershey, I brought with me that sense of endless possibilities. I used that energy to grow my tennis and running store. I thought the sky was the limit.

Over the next decade, trips to Key West were more of an escape from the very hard work that consumed me daily. Our business was almost as demanding as our roles as parents were. Time spent in Key West was time away from our everyday lives. It was time that also carried a lot of guilt. Guilt caused by not being present for our kids or being at the store. It was enjoyment with guilt.

Then our store collapsed financially, and it took many years before Sue and I could recover enough to even think of going to the Jersey shore for a vacation, let alone go to Key West. When we finally returned, I was almost fifty-two. My dreams had been scaled way back. The fact that we could pay all of our bills on time seemed to be enough of an accomplishment. But walking around Key West, I realized that I had to try one more time to get outside the limits that I had placed on myself. Something about observing all of the beauty and accomplishment that one sees while walking the many streets of Key West spoke to me. I returned with a new purpose. I grew my landscape company. I invested in several rental properties. I shifted the possibilities and removed some of my limitations.

As our finances grew healthier, our trips to Key West became a bit longer. Where we stayed in Key West became more comfortable. Our choices of which restaurants to patronize grew. It became a better and better vacation. I began to realize that if I lived my life as if it were a great vacation, it would not be enough for me. I was aging out of my landscape business. I did not wish to purchase more rental properties and increase my list of tenants. I also knew that I was not ready to completely retire. In Key West, I was enjoying a beautiful setting, great food, spectacular weather, tennis daily, and the opportunity to read almost a book a day. Even with all of that, I was ready to go home before our two weeks had come to a close. If I could not be satisfied to retire in Key West, how was I ready to retire in Hershey? That realization led me to begin a new venture, which, of course, is Cherry Blossom Creamery.

Now, as I walk around the same beautiful Key West, I ponder that decision. On one hand, I shudder at the amount of money that has already been spent and worry about the financial needs that this project still has. I worry about my body. It is a lot more fragile than it was two years ago when I began this project. This body always hurts. If it isn't the back, it is the feet, and I can always rely on my legs to be bothersome. If I don't work, all my aches present themselves ever more forcefully. When I am engaged, I can often forget about those same aches. If for no other reason but my general health, I do not think I have any alternative but to continue to work on this venture. I can only hope that I chose one that will not destroy our financial stability or be too strenuous for me to handle.

Chapter 18

Vacation is over. Two weeks of e-mails and regular mail have to be sorted and responded to. Every contractor has questions for me. Several of my tenants need something. How did I ever think I was bored in Key West?

On the bright side, all but one piece of equipment has arrived and been placed where I had indicated. There was more plumbing that needed to be finished than I had anticipated. Aside from the additional expense, that plumbing is not a concern. There is electrical work that needs to be completed next week, which I hope will not be too challenging. I have scheduled a final electrical inspection for next Tuesday. I am very concerned about this inspection. If we pass, I can ask for a final inspection. I am not certain if I want to wait a few days or try to have it done on the same day as the electrical inspection. I met with the site supervisor from Comcast and await further instructions as to when Comcast will install the internet.

I have been given several marketing possibilities. My plumber, Mike Leonard, sends a Valentine card every year to all of his almost five thousand customers. In the card is a $30.00 gift card to be used by his customer sometime in the next year. Mike has offered to enclose a second card for Cherry Blossom Creamery. This card entitles the recipient to buy one large ice cream, get one free. I will not make any money on this deal, and I had initially rejected the idea. After further thought, I realized that I was being given free access to a great local customer list. I also incurred no expense in the printing, as Mike was producing all of the cards. Nor was I paying anything for the mailing of those coupons. I reconsidered and gave the go-ahead to this promotion.

A second opportunity arose from my former employee and the owner of Livinglandesign. He had missed his Christmas deadline for giving many of his landscape customers some type of gift. He decided that he needed to do something to show his appreciation before spring arrived. He suggested a $20.00 gift card from Cherry Blossom Creamery. He would reimburse me as his customers used their Cherry Blossom gift card. All I needed to do was provide the coupons. I began working on those coupons immediately.

I also attended for the first time the Hershey Partnership breakfast. My wife, Sue, has represented the Hershey Art Association for many years, and that organization has been a part of the Partnership. The breakfast was crowded and fun. Maybe I made a couple of good contacts. More importantly, I have to make a decision on joining very quickly. The Partnership produces a Hershey Map that is given to tourists and to hotels, which lists businesses that are a part of the Hershey Partnership. I have about two weeks to decide before I run up against the map submission deadline.

I am certain that I want to be on the Hershey Map. It is not the expense that is keeping me from buying in. It is my inability to decide what to do with my store phone. Normally, any listing would have the store's phone number. That is where I begin to have doubts. I am not sure that I want a phone to be answered in the store. I do not think that customers are going to call ahead to order an ice cream cone. I think that the only phone calls I will receive will be solicitations, surveys, or people wanting to talk to my employees. If it is my stated goal to have my employees be engaged, friendly, and present, then I do not want them on the phone. I think I want all calls to go to voicemail, where there would be options to listen to store location, store hours, and maybe even flavor specials. Another option would be to leave a voicemail for the store manager.

Due to time constraints in producing the coupons for Livinglandesign and Mike Leonard Plumbing, my decision was made for me. I had no phone number to list. Instead, we listed the store address and the website, cherryblossomcreamery.com. If the long-anticipated Comcast install does not soon occur, my decision as to what will appear on the Hershey Map will be made for me as well.

Using our website as our contact point also has problems. We had reserved and purchased the domain for Cherry Blossom Creamery, but we had not done much work on the website. Making this a live website has now become a priority. Folks will be receiving coupons from Cherry Blossom Creamery very soon. If we do not have a functioning website, it will reflect poorly on our store. I have emailed Jon, the website designer, and explained our problem. He is asking for some content and some pictures so that he can get a bit of a website in place in the next few weeks.

I believe the questions, opportunities, and work that these different marketing possibilities presented are illustrative of how winding the road is to opening a new business. Upon returning from Key West, I thought that I would be spending the majority of my efforts on completing the installation of the equipment and preparing for a couple of inspections. I did spend time on those items, but the majority of my efforts this week were on getting Comcast installed, thinking about our phone system, investigating different marketing proposals, and sending information that will get our website active. Working on opening a new business is never a straight line, but instead a road filled with curves, cul-de-sacs, and unfortunately, some dead ends. The effort requires constant reprioritizing and quick pivots.

Chapter 19

Even though I was able to work on many items on my ever-growing to-do list, the one item that is still sitting on top of that list that I can not cross out is to secure an occupancy permit from Derry Township. I have been working on this item for over a year. It began with securing architectural drawings for my store. Immediately, we had to detour with a visit to Labor and Industry to grant me a variance for accessibility concerns. Addressing that accessibility brought me to a dead end. I needed to repave a parking lot that was already paved so that I could get the needed slope. Other than meeting a requirement, this money spent was of no use to my project. A building permit was finally issued.

We then had a Zoom meeting with the plan examiner, which resulted in some progress as a few of the more onerous requirements were relaxed. We entered a cul-de-sac. Although the plans did not indicate the need for additional reinforcing of the floor, the plan examiner zigged and zagged to the conclusion that I needed to reinforce my floor. Although I was unhappy at the extra expense, now that it has been completed, I find some comfort in the fact that my very heavy pieces of equipment are resting on a more secure floor. Plumbing, electrical, and mechanical all proceeded with few surprises, other than the constantly escalating cost. Inspections were completed for framing, rough electrical, and rough plumbing. Straight down the highway, we passed those inspections. All that is left is the final electrical and final inspection. My concern about the electrical inspection was well-founded. The inspector was concerned with the wire going above the ceiling and the method used for running the wire in the crawl space. We hit another dead end, we failed the first final electrical inspection.

My electrician, Ken, phoned our inspector and discussed what was needed. Ken made the necessary changes, and we scheduled a second final electrical inspection. This time, I had Ken there with me to meet with the inspector. Another dead end. Even though the inspector's initial concerns were rectified, the inspector found a few minor issues, such as a few missing ground faults and a lack of labeling the new electrical circuits. Ken volunteered to make the minor repairs right away, but the inspector had other places to go, so we once again had another dead end. We failed our second inspection. Two days later, the third inspection took place. It required at most ten minutes. Now we are heading down the shoulder of the highway with all of our preliminary inspections completed. We still have to pass the final inspection,

Which will be done by the same inspector, Mick, who was the inspector that we had worked with when the dueling levels came into play for the accessibility inspection several months ago. I am certain that he will find several items that will cause us further expense and delay. The inspection is scheduled for next week.

With so much still to get done, I needed to shift from my occupancy permit quest and work on other tasks. I selected and ordered our Cherry Blossom Creamery T-shirts, hats, and aprons. All of these items will serve as backup uniforms for our staff, as well as being available as merchandise for sale to our customers. I also ordered our staff golf shirts.

I was able to meet again with our point of sale representative. I wanted to simplify the way our customers paid for their ice cream. It is my goal that we make it as easy and quick as possible for our customers to order, receive their ice cream, and pay for their purchase. I also wanted the ability to offer gift cards, track loyalty rewards, and generate a few sales reports. I think we are almost there.

Capturing e-mails from our customers will be essential to effectively market changes in hours, days open, specials, and events. Lori, who is designing our point of sale system, introduced me to Terri, who is a representative of Constant Contact. It is my goal that customers who wish to be a part of our email marketing can easily sign up for this without our staff having to do anything when they are checking out at our register. Terri is coordinating with Jon, my website designer, to allow customers to go to our website and sign in for email marketing. Terri is also developing a Q code to make it simple for someone to become a part of our Cherry Blossom Creamery mailing list.

There are so many items to track. Many years ago, when I began my sporting goods store, all that seemed to be necessary to open the store was a landline telephone and a cash register. Now I need at least a Facebook presence, a Google account, several e-mail addresses, a Constant Contact account, a QR code, and a point of sale. It is my goal with this business for me to not manage by abdication but manage by accountability. Even with that goal in mind, I will welcome handing the social media component off to a properly trained associate as soon as I am able.

Mick, Derry Township's code enforcement officer, conducted what is termed a final inspection on Wednesday. He identified a few problem areas, including grab bars in the bathroom that were not properly located by a few inches to the left or to the right or to a vertical grab bar that was less than an inch too low. He also indicated that the fire extinguisher was not at the proper height. His biggest concern was some venting in the plumbing in the production room. Our inspection failed. Mick suggested that we attempt to schedule a second inspection the next day, as long as we are able to make the changes he noted. I called the township office immediately and was informed that the next appointment possible was the following Tuesday. Without the occupancy permit, I could not go forward with PA agriculture inspections. Another delay of a week.

Finally, a pleasant surprise. Thursday, the day after our failed inspection, I had a meeting with another of our vendors. We were determining what size tubs would work in our dipping cabinets when Mick walked into the store. He indicated that he needed to once again review the plumbing that he had been concerned about in his earlier inspection. After spending a bit of time doing this review, Mick decided that the plumbing was not ideal but passable. I then asked Mick if he would like to look at the other items that he had flagged. He said yes. He did the inspection and then asked to look at the crawl space. This request was outside his earlier inspection. I was concerned. He did ask a few questions while we viewed the space, but seemed to be satisfied with what he was viewing. Back to the store and a final signature on our building permit, and I now had an occupancy permit. It had taken eighteen months to arrive at this moment. I should have felt joyous, but instead, I was just tired.

Earlier in the day, I had made the assumption that the originally scheduled second final inspection would go well and that I would have an occupancy permit by the end of next Tuesday. With that time frame in mind, I reached out to Robert, my agriculture inspector. He explained that I would need to have two tests, each a week apart, for the soft serve machine and each of the two batch freezers. Before I could legally make ice cream, I needed two good tests. Thinking that I already was losing a week because of the second inspection, I pushed to have the new ice cream machines installed as soon as possible after that inspection. My desire was not altogether met. Rich was only able to schedule his installation and training for a week later. We now would be finishing the installation of my equipment on Tue Feb 28. If this date was going to work, I had a lot of coordinating to do. I needed to have my ice cream mix supplier deliver the soft serve and ice cream mixes sometime during the week before. It was essential that they were not frozen, as that would make them unusable, but also that they were not sitting in the refrigerator for too long, which could contribute to a bad test result. I also needed to contact and schedule a third-party lab testing group. They needed to sample the soft serve machine within a couple of days of its production and to have a sample of the batch freezer ice cream shortly after that ice cream had been produced. With a flurry of phone calls back and forth, I would have the necessary ice cream mixes by the middle of the week prior to testing. The testing lab agreed to get their samples on March 1, the day after our machines were to be installed.

My huge sigh of relief did not take long to be extinguished. The scheduled Comcast installation was also to happen on this very eventful day. My installer arrived, surveyed the situation, brought the cable from the back of the building to the and announced that he was finished. I asked him where the modem was. He said that it was his job to bring the cable, but it was my responsibility to phone customer service to schedule the final installation. By this time, I was getting very weary of final anything. He told me to phone my sales representative and order the final install. I proceeded to call Greta. She had not yet gotten to work. She did phone me several hours later, and the conversation went badly. It was not her job, nor did she know exactly who to contact to accomplish my goal. The number she gave me to call turned out to be fully automated. Since my cell phone was tied to our residential account, the robot was never able to access my new business account. After half an hour trying to outsmart the artificial intelligence on the other end, I gave up. I was ready to cancel the entire order. I was really contemplating using a cash register and dropping the point of sale system. I did not know if it was possible to have a landline phone installed, but I was getting ready to investigate that possibility. In a final effort for a final install, I once again called Greta, my sales representative. She sympathized with my plight and found a different number. Once an appropriate time had passed on hold, I did speak with a real person who was able to locate my installation order. She assured me that someone would get back to me and schedule the now final Comcast installation. There is a momentum that is built when opening a new business, which results in following the path that often stretches ahead. I am not certain that a year from now I would not be happier if I had decided to get a land line and a simple cash register. *I hope that is not the case.*

Chapter 20

The build-out of the store was reaching a critical stage. The majority of the work was finished, inspected and signed off. The plumbing, electrical, and mechanical systems were finished. What was left was a lot of small odds and ends that my brother-in-law was attempting to complete. He was working at a substantial disadvantage. My sister has been declining mentally for several years. She now wants to be with Rich wherever he goes. This is not a problem, as I certainly do not mind having my sister sit in the store while Rich works. The problem is that my sister gets bored and wants to return to her home. When Rich takes her home, she wants Rich to stay at home. If he does stay home, then the work will continue to be unfinished.

In just one week, we will be having the testing company stop at our store and pull samples from our soft serve machine. They will also want to have samples from our small and larger batch freezers. The areas that we are use to producing the ice cream that they will sample need to be clean. Very clean. This is not a concept that translates well to Rich. Rich is a great carpenter.

Rich is a great problem solver. Rich makes a mess. When he is finished for the day there is the random nail or screw. There is always sawdust or other dust. You do not want to eat off the floor of one of Rich's work sites, but we need to have the area clean enough that you might want to do just that, eat off the floor. I want to do a thorough cleaning of the production room. It is only three hundred square feet, but it has lots of heavy equipment with lots of areas that need cleaning. I do not want to begin this job until Rich finishes his work in the production room. He needs to hang five shelves, replace some screws, and install a diffuser in the heating system. I am certain that when I visit the store in the morning, not all of these tasks will be completed. My frustration was reaching a peak. I felt that I could not get a handle on any part of the store. The front dipping area still required the installation of our modem and our point of sale connection. This would require Rich to drill some more holes. The hallways in the back still needed shelves. That would cause more dirt. The very back room was a disaster. The electrician found significant rot in the far back wall. We needed to wait until our final inspection was complete before this problem was tackled. No need for the inspector to see this problem. The utility room needed painting. Most of all, that room was playing host to every tool that Rich owned and maybe some that were not even his. I felt that I had lost control of the schedule. I absolutely appreciated everything that my brother-in-law was doing for me, but I was ready to bring in someone else who could work longer hours and complete this job. My 3:30 AM musings were not pleasant.

Some mornings start out great. I walked into the production room and found the shelves hung and the heating vent closed. I wasn't sure about the screws. They all look pretty much the same to me. Rich had concentrated his efforts on this room, and I was thrilled to go on to the next step. I found cleaning supplies. I moved the equipment enough to get to the least accessible areas of the room. Using a clean sponge, I got on my hands and knees and did a great job of cleaning this one room.

I was ready to make ice cream in my small and friendly batch freezer. I had limited options as I did not have an overnight time frame to marinate any fruit. I chose coffee and butter pecan as the first flavors I would create in the new production room. I wanted to produce some fresh ice cream as I wanted to give this ice cream to the next two folks I would be meeting. The first recipient of the free ice cream was my screen printer/ embroiderer. I dropped off some samples, which were quickly consumed even though it was barely seven o'clock in the morning. Ice cream for breakfast just might work. I noted this as a possible promotion if I ever get the store opened.

I was given the opportunity to inspect the silk screen design. I made a few modifications and placed the order for our short-sleeved t-shirts. My second stop was with the embroidery department. The staff shirts that had been shown to me were out of my price range. We worked through some other options and arrived at shirts that I cannot afford, but were less expensive than the original ones. I placed the order.

The second set of ice cream samples will travel to Lewisberry, where I will get the opportunity to meet Donald Reeser. I have bombarded Don with questions via e-mail about the ice cream business, ranging from the difficult to the clearly idiotic. He has responded quickly with great information and shown extreme patience. I suggested that it might be great if I could come to his facility and steal his solutions to a bunch of my problems. Why Don has agreed to this is unclear, but I am not giving him much time to reconsider. I have made a list of questions that even I find daunting. I fear that the couple of cups of ice cream that I am transporting will in no way compensate Don for what I am asking of him.

Don's ice cream business has been around for over fifty years. He took over from his father and plans to continue the business for at least another five years. He is high energy and passionate about frozen custard. His business model is quite a bit different than mine. He is set up to serve huge numbers of customers with delicious soft serve ice cream, whether in a cone, cup, milkshake, or sundae. There are no dipping cases, hardening cabinets, or batch freezers. The ice cream is served in Styrofoam containers. Picnic tables are the seating choice. There is no space for inside seating as every available square foot is utilized either for storage or design. Even though I am attempting a far different concept, I did learn quite a bit from Don. We discussed types of hot fudge dispensers. He smartly offered that butterscotch worked best in a squeeze bottle. We discussed pricing and portion sizes. Most useful to me was his demonstration of a label maker. I bought one on the way home. It will save me from having to purchase premade labels at far greater cost and in quantities that I might never exhaust.

Don reminded me that I needed to reach out to Mike Geiger, who has been working in the ice cream business for the last forty years. Mike is an expert on cups, napkins, and other items I will need in my store. I have an appointment with him next week.

Another task has been completed. I now have an internet and phone connection. For this to happen, Comcast had to send a third technician to complete my install. This journey began with the site survey. Once that technician determined that, in fact, Comcast could install service, my account was passed to the cable installer. That task complete, the third person from Comcast now brought and installed the modem. I now had my much-delayed telephone number. All I needed was to purchase a land-line phone and set up my appropriate voicemail. I thought I was home free, but not the case. I registered Cherry Blossom Creamery and opened my account. When I attempted to record my own greeting for my voicemail, the old generic greeting was what still played. While attempting to do this, I had the foresight to ask Matt, yes, my old mower foreman, to be present. He was also unable to fix this problem. He called Comcast customer service and miraculously reached a live person who, upon investigating the problem, found that Comcast had neglected to do something on their end. The customer service person pressed the correct buttons, and I now had control of my voicemail.

Almost everything was now complete in the dipping/serving area in the front of the store. The continued construction has left a lot of dust and small debris. It was such a good feeling to spend several hours cleaning the dipping cases, the soft ice cream machine, the bae marie and most rewarding, the floor. The soda dispenser and the ice machine still require sanitizing before they can be operational.

The soda dispenser is one of the great unknowns. I do not know how to operate it. I don't know how to clean it. I do not know how to change any of the syrups or carbonators. I need to replace those unknowns with help from Coca-Cola before we open.

With a phone number in hand, I placed a sign beside our roadside sign advertising that we are now hiring. It has been a few days, but there has not yet been any response. I have made an employment offer to Matt, the same mower foreman. Matt has been extremely helpful in moving equipment, assembling shelves, removing shelves from other locations, and most importantly, helping me to understand more technological issues. It is a strange hiring decision. I am offering him the position of social media associate. I do need help with this task. I think Matt can do the job as I have outlined it in the job position description. What is problematic is that Matt had worked for me for seven years as a Greenscapes employee. He was an excellent employee, but will that familiarity with me hinder his acceptance of what I am attempting to do with this new company? Will he buy into the premise that we will have a system for everything we do? I expect everyone to do things in the same way. It is not that we cannot change how we do things, but that change will originate from improving how we do particular tasks. Any changes will be updated in our operations manual. Will I be able to monitor and make certain that those systems are adhered to, or would it be easier to allow someone like Matt, whom I have a lot of trust in, to just go off on his own? If he did, the results would probably be the same, but the how to do things would no longer be consistent. This will test my commitment to building a company in a different manner than I have ever done before.

The company that I purchased the large batch freezer and the soft serve machine from arrived to both install those machines and train me in their operation. Once again, I asked Matt to attend this meeting. The soft serve machine, after it is assembled, is relatively simple to operate and delivers a great-tasting and consistent product. It is the clean-up and reassembly that is anything but simple. Observing the technician do this task, I am certain that I will never get this machine back together. Once the testing company completes the two tests necessary, Matt and I are going to attempt to clean and put that machine back together again. It is our intention to both write easy-to-understand directions and to supplement that effort with step-by-step photographs.

I will need to wait a few days to undertake that endeavor. I did ask the testing company to test my meadow tea concentrate for bacteria contamination. The concentrate had been in my freezer for six months. It had been thawed, properly diluted and sampled by the tester. The results came back as no bacteria. Hoping that all of our other tests fare as well.

Chapter 21

The Hershey Partnership is an organization of businesses and service clubs that constitute what Hershey would term our Chamber of Commerce. With the payment of yearly dues, a partner is entitled to attend a once-a-month breakfast, where, along with good food, there is a sharing of information about your organization. It is also a great method of networking. As another benefit, you receive a listing in the visitor's guide that the Partnership, along with a few other groups, produces, which is distributed to some of our large number of tourists that find their way to Hershey each year. I proudly joined the group and gave my first two-minute speech about Cherry Blossom Creamery. There seemed to be a good bit of enthusiasm for an ice cream store in Hershey, but underlying that enthusiasm was a shared concern. The concern that every business shared was the ability to find employees

As we are very close to opening, that concern was at the top of my mind. My voicemail has not been entirely quiet. It is now the weekend, and I have four messages indicating some interest in employment. Upon returning all of the calls, I am directed to their voicemail. I left messages. No reply so far. I do share the concerns of my new friends at the Partnership. Will I have anyone to work at my store? The question that those first applicants left on the voicemail was: What is our pay scale? I want to bring every new employee in at a base rate. It is my hope that the base rate will be augmented by an additional amount as the employee signs off on the job requirements for a particular job description. For example, once the employee completes the training for a sales associate, that employee will receive a small raise. As that employee completes the training to become a cleaning associate, that employee will receive another small raise. This concept continues as the employee masters other jobs, whether they be employee training and retention or a clean-up specialist. With the additional responsibilities will come additional compensation. If this concept is to work, I need the base pay to be low enough that Cherry Blossom Creamery can remain profitable, but high enough to at least interest any applicant to learn more about our company and its somewhat unique compensation plan. To complicate the question of what we are paying is the matter of tips. Although I am not certain how large a factor tips will be, I am fairly confident that it will add at least two to three dollars per hour to our employees' hourly pay. With all that in mind, I believe I will answer the question of starting pay as a range of possibilities and hope that I will have the opportunity to meet with the applicant and explain our situation.

You never know where help in solving a problem will come from. The label maker that I had purchased was confounding my poor attempts at producing labels. I asked my daughter, Meghan, if she had any experience with this type of machine at her veterinary clinic. She said no, but bring the machine to the clinic as she was certain that one of her vet techs would be able to help. Once again, she was right. Within a few minutes, the major mysteries of my new toy were unraveled. Back in my office, I was able to produce labels to properly mark my new ice cream containers. The ice cream that was going into those containers was being produced by my new large batch freezer. The operation and cleaning of this machine were similar enough to my small batch freezer that I was making ice cream with a very short learning curve.

The resultant ice cream was both excellent in flavor and more plentiful than I had foreseen. Once I made a few batches, I realized that I needed to recalculate my costs for the manufactured ice cream. The cost per pint had been reduced sufficiently to allow me to explore the possibility of offering quarts as well for sale in my take-out freezer. Previously, I felt that the cost of a quart of my ice cream would be so high that it would not be attractive. More importantly, it would reflect that our ice cream was just too expensive. With the new calculations, I am hopeful that our take-out freezer will be able to offer even better options.

I postponed ordering the furniture that I need to finish the store. The delay was caused by several factors. I reviewed furniture websites and could not find anything that I fell in love with. I was also so hesitant to commit money to this purchase. In the hope that I could spend a fraction of what I knew I was going to spend, I searched an auction site and a used restaurant supply house and found very inexpensive furniture that I did not like, nor that fit the theme of our store.

Finances are something that I have not mentioned a lot until now. Before I began, I had a sense of what it would take to make this adventure a reality. The major pieces of equipment, such as the dipping cabinets, the reach-in freezer, the reach-in refrigerator, the hardening cabinet, the refrigerated work stations, and the small and large batch freezers, all had a price tag that I could calculate. The supply chain issues and inflation that occurred as we entered the post-pandemic era added significant additional costs. The development of a handicap parking space and the reinforcing of the floors were unexpected costs that were incurred in order to obtain our occupancy permit. Repairing the back storage room now that we are getting close to opening has just added insult to injury. It has been my goal to open this store with no outstanding debt. I have seen firsthand how having significant debt adversely affects a business. I had to close a good business which had not been careful in incurring debt. Cherry Blossom Creamery has used all of the money that I had accumulated from the sale of my landscape business. It has also used all of the proceeds of the sale of one of our commercial properties. It has also used money from our personal savings. Unfortunately, this hasn't been quite enough capital. I have had to utilize a portion of our home equity loan, which will mean that I will not open this store debt-free. With this in mind, it was extremely difficult to spend the five thousand dollars to obtain the furniture that would fit with my store's concept. But I have to. I spent and designed so much that it seems penny-wise and pound-foolish not to finish the concept. I placed the order. Bad news, it will be four weeks until delivery. If I am opening the store by the end of March, it will be without chairs and tables.

Once the furniture was ordered, I had hoped that I would be leaving my charge card safely in my wallet. I was not correct. I realized that I still needed a lot of items. I had been so focused on how to produce superior ice cream and how to organize the dipping space that I neglected some essential items. This oversight was made clear to me when I met Mike Geiger. The two of us traveled north of Lewisburg to meet with and tour W A Dehart. This is a huge operation. Almost everything that could be thought of and utilized in making frozen desserts was in the mammoth warehouse. Mike spent several hours pointing out items that I would need immediately, and then the items that he thought I would find useful in the future. I needed two sizes of cones, three sizes of cups, many toppings, some variegates, other syrups, napkin dispensers, napkins, and the list goes on. Aside from my charge card getting more exercise, I also realized that I had not made space for cones, or cups, or hot fudge, or spoons, or two types of straws.

As soon as I returned to my store, I began rearranging the area behind the dipping cases. I realized that I needed another work table for the hot fudge dispenser. I moved the bae marie and was able to squeeze the work table in the newly created space. I purchased a cabinet that Rich hung above the ice machine. This would be where the supplies could be kept for serving the ice cream. We found a place to hang the waffle display case and the drink cup holder. I ordered two cone dispensers. I believe we have a spot for them when they arrive. I had always thought that I had plenty of space in the serving area. Now I wish I had a bit more space. Somehow, we will have to work with what is there.

The repairs to the back room are complete. Rich has consolidated all of his work tools to the room that we are going to use as our sanitation room. With most of the store approaching its opening layout, I spent a satisfying Sunday morning sweeping and hand scrubbing the back area of the store. With the shelves in place, I was able to relocate items from the middle of the floor and the production room onto those shelves. It is finally looking like a shop.

The second lab test results came back on Friday. We did great. Both the batch freezers and the soft serve machine passed. My food inspector had told me that two good tests were all that he required for him to inspect our store. He is scheduled for next Wednesday afternoon. At the onset of this adventure, I began working on the three big concepts that needed to be completed in order to someday open Cherry Blossom Creamery. The months spent making ice cream in my test kitchen somewhat completed the how to make ice cream portion. The months of modifying plans, getting variances, and filling other requirements have resulted in obtaining an occupancy permit. If on Wednesday, Cherry Blossom Creamery passes the agricultural inspection, Cherry Blossom Creamery will be able to make and sell ice cream. I have been asked by several of my friends if I could go back two years, would I have attempted to create this store? At this moment, I am tired, financially poorer, and very worried about the operation of the store. I do know that someone who had to make a living from this venture immediately would have had a very difficult time weathering the delays and additional costs that I have worked through.

Our inspector came, saw, and issued a frozen desserts license and a food establishment license. Now all I have to do is find staff, train staff, make the needed ice cream, finalize the point of sale system, order and receive all the miscellaneous items such as cups, cones, toppings, etc. When I survey the enormous amount of items that need to be taken care of, I am also very aware that my concept of this store being able to run itself requires me not to lose sight of the documentation and training that I need to do and not fall into the trap of either me doing too much or relying on special employees doing things that are outside of the system. I also need to give myself some slack, as somehow we have to be able to serve ice cream soon. Working on the structure of the business will have to be dealt with lightly until I can catch my breath.

CHAPTER 22

It has been a pleasure to work with so many of the companies that I have used to get to this point in getting ready to open my store. Tim at Commercial Refrigeration returns my calls immediately and looks for solutions to whatever problem crops up with his equipment. Rich at Love's has been a steady resource. Mike at DeHart has acted as my personal encyclopedia of knowledge. Ed at Valley Farms has been great at getting me the finest ice cream mix possible. Alas, not all the companies that I have dealt with match the service of those companies already mentioned.

Two weeks ago, I made the difficult decision to spend a lot of money on chairs and tables. I reasoned that if I did not purchase the furniture that I wanted, I would not be able to have the look that I desired for the store. I placed that order with a large internet resource, Restaurantfurniture. I was pleasantly surprised when they notified me that the order was going to ship two weeks earlier than originally thought. The order arrived packed on a skid. The driver brought the skid to our back door. The number of packages matched his bill of lading. I signed, and the driver was on his way. We brought the first package inside. We hurriedly unpacked the box, only to find two chairs that were the correct style but the wrong color. Instead of light blue, they were light green. I quickly realized that all of the boxes that contained the thirty chairs were marked light green.

I phoned Restaurantfurniture and was shuttled to customer service. Ashley was courteous. I recounted the color error. I expected that she would offer a method to return the incorrect chairs. Instead, she informed me that quality assurance needed to see pictures of the chairs. She also noted that I needed to forward pictures of the chairs inside all the many packages, as sometimes the color of the furniture does not match what is written on the box. Her final instructions to me were to keep the chairs safe. I tried to explain that they were in my store, but that they were occupying needed space. I then asked how long it would be before some resolution of this problem would present itself. She volunteered that I would hear from quality assurance within forty-eight hours. Matt took the needed photos and sent them to customer service. I phoned first thing the following morning to be certain that the photos arrived. I was assured that they had arrived safely. I asked once again when I could expect a resolution to my problem. Within forty-eight hours was the reply.

More than two days passed without any follow-up from Restaurantfurniture. I once again had the pleasure of speaking with another customer service representative. He informed me that the company had sent an email to me and they were awaiting my reply. I told him no such email had ever arrived. I even checked my spam folder while we were on the phone. He resent the email, which eventually got to me. While I was waiting, I quizzed him as to how much longer this process would take. He answered that the timing was up to quality assurance, but felt it would be resolved within the next couple of days. I was frustrated and did not want to wait another few days. I requested to speak to his supervisor. He informed me that that would not be possible. I asked, do you not have a supervisor? He indicated that although he had a supervisor, that person did not speak to customers like me. By this time, the long-awaited email had arrived. It asked if I had requested a sample of the product order before placing my order. I answered with a simple no and sent that reply.

Later that day, I received an email stating that I had agreed to the conditions of sale. In those conditions, the furniture company is not responsible for deviations in color or wood stain. It was my responsibility to have asked for a sample before ordering. The email stated that I received exactly what I had ordered. There is nothing that this company was going to or wished to do to correct my problem. This seemed incredible. I once again looked at their website. The chairs on their website that were identified as light blue still had not changed color and looked, in fact, like light blue. My confirmation of my order clearly stated light blue. The boxes they came in were clearly marked light green. The chairs that I received matched the light green color that was clearly marked on the boxes. Instead of doing the right thing and offering some method to correct their mistake, they choose to hide behind the fine print in their ordering procedure. I have few options. I am going to speak with my credit card company and determine if I can dispute the charge.

Even if I were to win my case about the erroneous color shipped, I still need to decide what to do with the chairs. I really want blue. I asked my painter to investigate the possibility and the expense of painting the chairs the color I desire. It looks like we could go that way. If we decide to do this, I will even have chairs that totally match my color scheme. It is becoming apparent to me that this chair color dispute is allowing me to not worry about the myriad of items that I must take care of if I am ever to open. The chairs represent something in my comfort zone. They may be an annoying portion of my comfort zone, but they are still in my comfort zone. The other issues, such as finding enough capable employees, or determining the proper temperature for dipping cabinets, or arriving at proper sizes, prices, labels, and portions, are all way out of my comfort zone. I need to make a decision about how important getting a blue chair really is. I need to let go of this problem so that I can focus on all the problems that I find myself uncomfortable working on.

The chair dispute continued for many months. The charge card company decided that restaurantfurniture had processed my purchase correctly. The supporting documents that led to this decision were remarkable. Restaurantfurniture indicated that I had made no attempt to return the incorrect chairs prior to disputing the charge on my credit card. This enraged me as I had talked to several so-called customer service representatives immediately, and several days after receiving the chairs. I wrote back to my bank detailing this misrepresentation and requesting that the charge be placed back in dispute. By this time, two things occurred. I have already paid the amount that had been placed on my charge card, and I have unpacked and used the mint green chairs. We needed to have furniture if we were going to open. We painted a wall the same color as the mint green chair to make everything look great in the store. Financial compensation is no longer my first concern. It is the principle that a company can misrepresent, then lie when confronted about that misrepresentation, that caused me to continue to press this issue. Finally, the charge card dispute was denied by my credit card company. My only recourse would be to begin a lawsuit or to accept the unfairness of the situation. I realize that my readers are probably not going to ever need the type of furniture that this company sells, but I beg them, if they ever would think of ordering from restaurantfurniture.net, to not do so.

Chapter 23

Everything about this adventure seems to be getting smaller. The excitement that I thought I would feel now that Cherry Blossom Creamery is about to open has changed to, at times, anxiety and at other times dread. The pressure of all those things that I don't know how to accomplish has forced me to narrow my focus, forcing me to ignore many items on my to-do list. Instead, I have had to spend time training employees on the size of the scoop when serving a regular dish of ice cream or how to properly sanitize a tabletop. Determining how to properly label the ingredients in our take-along pints and quarts or how to enter a gift card in our point of sale system has greatly narrowed my vision to the ordinary.

At least at this moment in this journey, I find myself reducing what I had set out to do with this business. I just need to open. In order to do this, I may need to reduce my hours as I can not find enough employees. I have reduced our number of toppings. I have eliminated sundaes and even milkshakes until we can get comfortable with our daily tasks. Instead of my mind entertaining new combinations of flavors or the wild combinations of our own snacks, I continue to be mired in the minutia of attempting to open. Even more damaging to the long-term success of this business has been my inability to document all the tasks necessary to be done. I am not building sustainable systems, but instead the operation of the store will rely on me working constantly, or I will have to depend on the idiosyncratic work of others that I trust.

This has even impacted the rest of my life outside of Cherry Blossom Creamery. It is spring, and I have barely noticed the flowers and trees in their full beauty. It is as if the acknowledgment of that beauty feels disloyal to accomplishing my tasks. I barely make any of my favorite meals at home, as I am tired of kitchen-style work when I do get home. I have spent no time on my final stain glass panel, which lies languishing in the stain glass room. I feel mocked by my garden and the absence of seeds and plants being planted there. Everything about my life feels constricted. As powerful as this feeling is, this sensation can not be only mine. It has to be common to many individuals who venture into starting their own business. Do I have the energy to hurdle this large bump in the road? Will this be how Cherry Blossom Creamery joins so many other businesses as merely a place to work? A place to work all the time? Or can I reclaim the excitement and creativity that I had originally approached this venture with? At this moment, I have no idea how this will play out.

Even though my sense of adventure seems to be shrinking, there is much to do before we open. Employees were always going to be a concern in this present economy. My sign indicating that we are hiring has produced several prospects. Most of them are between fourteen and eighteen years old. I did get a couple of women that I hired during their application interview. Both are in their late thirties and indicate that they have significant availability. Interviewing the kids has been surprising, as they present themselves in a very positive and intelligent manner. I have offered positions to everyone whom I interviewed. Their schedule, which includes athletics, school productions, dance, and family vacations, is making scheduling extremely difficult.

I have scheduled training sessions for all the hires. Matt has been gracious enough to work with the new hires. He has more food experience than I have, as he has worked in pizza shops for many years. We need to learn the correct procedures for sanitary handling of cones, cups, spoons, etc. We need to be consistent in our scoop sizes in all four of our sizes, including kids', regular, large, and extra large. Although ice cream is not sold by weight, Matt and I found it to be helpful for the kids to weigh their different-sized dips so that they could better understand serving sizes.

Learning portion control means wasting a good bit of ice cream. I am unwilling to allow our trainees to scoop our homemade ice cream while learning. Instead, I purchased gallons of Green's ice cream, which I then put in the appropriate tubs and used this ice cream for teaching purposes. I could feel okay about throwing that ice cream away when we had finished the training session. Using the soft serve machine and the soda dispenser is all a part of the training. I was just as much a part of the training as our kids, as I have no restaurant experience. The point of sale system has not yet been installed. We might have to have a separate training session to master that bit of technology.

Once the point of sale system was installed, it was only I who needed an extra training session. It is something I am not comfortable with. To illustrate, I had been more or less using the system for a week when one of our ice cream kids, Avery, came to work for her first shift. I attempted to demonstrate the system and very shortly got bogged down and confused. Avery looked at the screen and quietly said I think I got this. She then cleared the mess I had made and proceeded to be able to cash out customers with no difficulty.

I use the term ice cream kids because that is my workforce. The two older hires that I felt great about did not work out. One of them kept cancelling her training session times, until she finally informed me that this was not the opportunity she was looking for. The other never returned my calls or e-mails to attempt to schedule training sessions. She just disappeared. I am approaching opening night with only inexperienced teenagers, Matt, my former mowing foreman, me, and my wife.

With the help of Matt and Andy, one of the fathers of our ice cream kids, the soft serve machine is ready. My wife, Sue, has made some attractive signs showing our prices and toppings. I have made more handcrafted ice cream to further fill the dipping cabinets. Cherry Blossom Creamery does not have a professional signboard, or an assortment of snacks, or a stain glass mural, but it is time to open.

It is three o'clock on Thursday, March 31, 2023, and Cherry Blossom Creamery will open. I know we do not have employees who are experienced enough in serving ice cream to be competent. I know that I am very unsure as to how to manage a workforce that has an average age of sixteen, with none of our employees above the age of eighteen. This is not the management concept that I had envisioned. I thought that I would have two or three older employees who would be the store managers. The kids would take direction from those employees. I am opening with no management structure. If this is how we continue to operate, I am certain that we will fail. Sometimes it is so good to be wrong. As I would find out, the kids found their way. Not reporting to a manager forced the employees to do their own problem-solving. They became more invested in the business than they ever would have if they were constantly following directions. How well the store operated with the kids in charge was the biggest and best surprise of opening Cherry Blossom Creamery.

Opening night is akin to attending your own funeral, but much happier. There is a steady flow of customers that my very young staff and I greet with enthusiasm. Most of the folks coming into the creamery are friends or acquaintances of Sue and me. Our closest friends came to support and view the madness that is this concept. Just like attending a funeral, everyone will not speak ill of my ice cream adventure, regardless of their possible misgivings. I had little concept as to how to serve customers, but I began, like my staff, to improve in our dipping techniques. It was great to see so many people who felt that they should support this venture.

Now that so many of the customers on our first night were friends, will there be any customers that we don't know on Friday? Will there be anyone visiting our store on our second night? I didn't need to worry. Our sales were greater than on Thursday. More importantly, the number of customers known to me personally was a much smaller percentage. Saturday and Sunday continued to show better sales numbers. Customers told us how much they enjoyed the ice cream, which was gratifying. Their most consistent complaint was that we were not open enough hours. Can we find enough employees, and can we make enough ice cream to allow us to open more hours?

If our mix of product sales could change so that some of our sales were from products that did not require us to make handmade ice cream, it would allow us to do a little less work while attaining our revenue numbers. I purchased a soft serve machine in the hope that it would allow all of our customers, but particularly children, to have an alternative to our handmade ice cream. I may be attempting to fulfill a need that isn't there. After one week, we have sold almost no soft serve. Even more distressing was that what was in the soft serve machine needed to be thrown out in preparation for cleaning and sanitizing the unit for the following week. It is only one week in, but I am feeling very uneasy about my decision to have soft serve.

Closing on Sunday means that the next three days, Cherry Blossom Creamery will not be open. I need to find a bunch of supplies for both serving and producing ice cream. I need to commit myself to continued training and monitoring the ice cream kids. They did a good job for the first four days. They were enthusiastic, friendly, and engaged, but not terribly competent. We will continue to work on that.

Many times, people come into your life when you most need them. One of my good friends and, for a short while, a former employee, phoned me. She had a stain glass question. After asking and receiving limited help from me, I thought she would mention my ice cream store. I asked her if she was going to give me a hard tíme about this venture, and she indicated that she had no idea that it was I who was opening Cherry Blossom Creamery. After much joking, I asked her about her daughters, who I knew might be at the right age for my staff. Rachel indicated that the older daughter, Abby, had just quit her job and might be interested in part-time work. Abby and I soon got together. To my surprise, Abby had worked for four years at Rita's ice cream. Abby began working with me within days. Although she had not been scooping ice cream at Rita's, she understood so much about the frozen dessert store. She knew how to make milkshakes, a skill none of our staff possessed. She was also eager to help me make ice cream on one of the days we were closed. A second pair of hands is so crucial for getting higher production. On our first day together, we made over twenty gallons of ice cream that included six different flavors. Abby, at nineteen, is now our oldest ice cream kid.

Our second Thursday that we are open is approaching, and my stress level is high. I have not slept well for the last weeks. I am so exhausted that I fall asleep easily, but I wake about 1:00 o'clock and then I either lie there worrying and unable to return to sleep, or I sit and read for the next several hours. At some point, I get up, realizing that I am still more tired than I want to be and more anxious than I thought I would be.

As we get through the next three days, I can see considerable improvement in our staff competency. Adding Abby has certainly helped. I have been worried that we would not get enough customers. Then I am worried that we can not take care of too many customers. The flow of customers has been steady, with a bit of a major rush on Saturday. All three days had increases in volume over the prior week. Sunday is Easter, and I have decided, after much thought, to be open. For the first three hours of the Easter shift, we should have been closed. I was just about to close when a steady stream of customers began to appear. Our volume was more like a Thursday night instead of a Sunday, but we had a fair number of new ice cream customers getting the opportunity to try our ice cream. We did not get the soft serve machine running as we had difficulty getting the mix that weekend. It did not seem to matter; no one was asking for soft serve. That worry continues.

Chapter 24

The local paper, The Hummelstown Sun, wanted to write an article about Cherry Blossom Creamery. Monday, their reporter and photographer met me at the store. The article appeared in the Thursday edition. The article was complimentary, and quite a few customers commented that they were visiting our store because they had read about it in the Sun. One of the flavors that they had mentioned was Key Lime Pie. We completely ran out of that flavor by Saturday. In fact, our sales for the week had really picked up. By Sunday evening, our to-go freezer was nearly empty. Along with Key Lime Pie, we had sold out of eight other flavors. It is time for Abby and me to produce a lot more ice cream.

Our customers continue to want the store to be open more hours. I believe the limiting factor will be whether we can produce enough ice cream and if we can drive more business to the soft serve. On this, our third Sunday, we offered fifty cents off any size soft serve. It generated some sales, but soft serve continues to be only a small percentage of our total sales.

I am beginning to think that we might have enough competent employees to serve an increasing number of customers. My sleep has improved. Exhaustion and a little less worry have allowed me to sleep beyond the middle of the night.

What I do now understand better is just how much ice cream we need to make in order to keep our dipping cases and freezers filled. I have gotten into a bit of a routine, which is comforting and somewhat efficient. On Mondays, I determine what ice creams I should make for the coming weekend. I note what is needed from the restaurant supply stores, as well as ingredients such as strawberries, mangos, pecans, walnuts, etc. I take a drive to the supply stores and to Trader Joe's, which has quite a few of the difficult-to-find items. I might also stop at the local grocery store depending on my list. Price variations are so large on some of the items that the extra stop or two is quite worth the time spent. Once I get everything unloaded and placed in their proper spots, I leaf through the recipes and see what needs to be marinated, chopped, or pureed. While I am reviewing my ice cream recipes, my order from DeHart usually arrives and is sitting in our seating area. That order includes most of our paper supplies as well as ice cream toppings and sanitation supplies.

On Tuesday, my order of ice cream mix, soft serve mix and whipped cream arrives, and the driver has put it in the large refrigerator if I am not there. Often, I am making a small batch of ice cream in the morning, thus making me available to meet with the Valley Farm's driver. Tuesday afternoon, I begin the prep of fruit, nuts, crackers, or chocolate that we will use on Wednesday.

Wednesday, my helper, Abby, and I make as much ice cream as we can. I try to have the labels for the take-out lids made ahead of time, which also determines the number of take-out containers we will dip for each flavor. I have chosen the order in which we will make the ice cream, attempting not to have to clean the ice cream machine more often than is absolutely necessary. Our goal is to pack pints and quarts for the display freezer while producing tubs of the different flavors for the dipping cabinet. The pace is quick. We have to pay close attention to how long we are processing a batch. We need to monitor how long a finished tub is in the hardening cabinet, as we need to be able to dip this into our take-out containers before it becomes frozen too solid. Once all the ice cream that we just made is in the hardening cabinet, all that is left to do is clean all the utensils and the batch freezer.

Thursday, I might make a small batch of ice cream. My major job is to transfer the tubs of ice cream that we just produced on Wednesday into either the storage freezer, the display freezer, or the dipping case. Any product that we need in the dipping cases must first be filled from the older product, if possible. I have learned a lesson in transferring very cold ice cream. I now wear gloves. Weeks ago, I did not and had a case of frostbite on three of my fingers. Fortunately, this mistake only served as a warning and has done no permanent damage to my fingers. The hardening cabinet is at forty degrees below zero. That is really cold. Now it is Thursday, and it is time to open for our fourth week.

I do not know how to determine if we are doing well. It seems customers come even if the weather is not ideal. That is, until there are blowing winds, heavy rains, and a severe thunderstorm warning in effect.

I now know that no customers visit during that time. Saturday had all of those conditions until near 5 o'clock. Sales were non-existent, but the weather improved marginally, and people began to line up. It was not a good Saturday, but it ended better than I had hoped.

An unexpected personal event has forced my emphasis to turn to getting the very young and inexperienced staff ready to be able to open, close, and operate Cherry Blossom Creamery without my presence. A memorial service for my wife, Sue's, brother-in-law is going to be conducted over Memorial Day weekend in Indiana. We will be away for three days. Days that I am certain will be some of the busiest days yet for our store. In preparation for our trip, I am forcing myself to be absent during closing so that they can perform their checklist and we can determine where our problems lie. Due to their school schedules, it is difficult to have them open as we do so before they can get there. I need to have them practice on weekends. A bit of a shift in my scheduling needs to happen if this is to occur. Although I am apprehensive about leaving these many days this early, I choose to view this as an opportunity. I am viewing this as a blessing, forcing more structure for our store and beginning to strive for the overriding goal of Cherry Blossom Creamery being self-sustaining.

Six weeks in and I think are sales numbers have plateaued. The four days that we are open each week seem to result in the same amount of revenue generated. One week we have a great Saturday with a bad Thursday, while the next week we have our best Thursday ever, but a very slow Sunday. I realize that it is nowhere near peak ice cream season, but I have some concerns. I was certain that we would increase our sales each week. I have put more staff on and stayed open an hour later. I felt that we needed the extra staff as I anticipated higher sales, but for the past three weeks, our revenue has been flat, resulting in only an increase percentage of employee costs. I am unsure how to schedule staff as we move through the remainder of May.

On the positive side, our Google reviews, which have been totally unsolicited, continue to be stellar, five-star. My vague understanding of the internet indicates that this will help drive more business our way.

Chapter 25

I lost a turtle today. It is Tuesday, following the seventh weekend that we have been open. Except for a few years when I was in college and living in an apartment, I have had turtles as pets since I was ten years old. A dozen years ago, my landscape company constructed a beautiful stone twenty-by-forty-foot curved turtle pen. The enclosure offers both sun and shade as well as a constantly flowing self-contained rock fountain. The gate is wrought iron and even has a turtle motif at the bottom of it. Once the pen was built, I applied and received permission to adopt four Russian tortoises from the Long Island Turtle Rescue. I had to send the rescue photos and a statement from a veterinarian that I was equipped, particularly in the winter, to properly care for the adoptees. Russian tortoises do not hibernate, thus requiring a heated, properly lit home for the winter. I had just such a place in the basement of my commercial building. With all the proper facilities in place, the turtle rescue deemed my situation adequate. I soon received a UPS air shipment of my four tortoises.

Over the years, I have had occasion to rescue a few other turtles. Friends know that I love and care for turtles, so when an injured or misplaced turtle comes into their lives, I am their first phone call. Since none of my friends have the proper facility or do they have the desire to keep these turtles, I will keep them if I determine that I can be a good home for them.

Sadly, this past winter, Lala, one of my original Russian tortoises, stopped eating, and I was unable to change that dire situation. She died. This left me with Hershel, Vienna, and Gino. I also had the other turtles in my turtle pen.

The week prior to Tuesday was incredibly hectic. The preceding Friday evening, my old Subaru had been rear-ended while I was waiting in a long line of cars at a red light. Other than a bit of stiffness in my back, I was unhurt. The same could not be said for my car. The car needed to be towed to a holding lot. Ironically, I was going to trade this car the next week for a much newer and lower mileage Subaru.

Now I was in conversations with my insurance company, the other driver's insurance company, that company's adjuster, and the car dealer that I had planned to trade my car with. All of these folks wanted some information from me, and most importantly, a bit of my time. Time was not in abundance this week. Even though I am out of the landscape business, I still love plants. That love of plants is expressed by planting quite a few annuals and tropicals at my house, my daughter's veterinary practice, my other daughter's short-term rental, and most extravagantly at Cherry Blossom Creamery. I even have a neighbor who owns an insurance office that I plant flowers for each spring. In order to do this massive planting, I need to buy a lot of plants. For that reason, I receive a once-a-year delivery from a great greenhouse near Longwood

Gardens. They sent me an email informing me that the delivery, which would fill a lot of my driveway, was to come on the Friday preceding this Tuesday. Fortunately, the order arrived early in the morning, which was still hours before my auto accident.

Monday, I was in full planting mode. Every flat of flowers that I could get into the ground was one less that needed to be watered twice a day, sitting in my driveway. Monday is also a day that Cherry Blossom Creamery has needs of its own. If I am going to produce ice cream on Wednesday, I need to do some shopping and other prepping for Wednesday. The pace of work was brutal, but Monday was now behind me.

Tuesday started the same way. There was too much planting to do. I had too many tasks to accomplish for Cherry Blossom Creamery. Returning phone calls about the car accident and fielding inquiries regarding Cherry Blossom Creamery had me in a high state of anxiety. I was certain that I was never going to complete the plantings, which was keeping me from being able to focus on the business that I was trying to open. I must have taken a moment to go inside the turtle pen to fill the bird feeder that is located there while loading some flowers into my truck. A few hours later, I returned to my house only to see that the gate to the turtle pen was slightly ajar. I immediately checked to see if any of my turtles had escaped. Five of the six were still happily in the pen. Gino, one of the Russian tortoises, was nowhere to be found. I began a thorough search, ever expanding from the open gate. I spent an hour walking up and down the alley, peering into neighbors' yards, hoping to spy Gino. No joy. I mentioned my lost turtle to any neighbor that I encountered.

I know it is only a turtle, but I had volunteered to care for and protect this animal. I had done so for the last dozen years. Now it was because of my inattentiveness that I had probably doomed this charge of mine to either being run over, or being attacked by a dog, or a neighbor finding it and attempting to keep it as a pet not knowing that it will not hibernate on it's own thus dooming it to a slow and cruel death. This episode had made me stop and slow down. What I was attempting to accomplish was a lot. I needed to realize that not everything will get done when I desire it to. If plants die in the driveway, I can afford the loss. If we do not make all the ice cream on Wednesday that I would like, Cherry Blossom will remain open. The car situation will be resolved. I began this as an adventure. Somehow, it has morphed into a job with a lot of responsibilities. Both my turtle and my wife have lately reminded me that I am not enjoying myself. It is time to change that trajectory. If the loss of Gino forces me to face that truth, then at least something positive will come of it.

Wednesday afternoon, I climbed the outside steps that go right by the turtle pen. As is my custom, I looked in to see how many of the little guys were up and about. I did a double-take. There were three Russian tortoises. Gino was back. Had he climbed the stone wall to join his friends? No, I checked my voicemails and there was a message from my neighbor informing me that she had found Gino in her yard and had returned the wandering turtle to the pen. I immediately grabbed some greens from my refrigerator and some cantaloupe, and the turtles and I shared a celebratory homecoming for Gino. My guilt had been released. I hope the lesson that I had taken from this episode has not been lost.

Chapter 26

Tips from nowhere

My absence from Cherry Blossom Creamery, which had occupied much of my thoughts, took place as planned over Memorial Day weekend. There was no choice in the timing or my attendance at it as it was a life celebrating memorial for Sue's sister's husband, Phil. I had spent much of the month of May worrying about the opening and closing of the store, not to mention the daily operation of it. I did not receive a single phone call during the three days. When I returned, the store looked clean, reasonably well stocked and ready for our final bonus day of the holiday weekend, Memorial Day.

The only troubling item was that Matt, who had checked in a few times during my absence, approached me with a question from the crew. They thought they would like to split the cash tips at the end of each shift. The way I had been doing the cash tips was to determine the total hours that all of the employees worked in that week. Then I calculated each employee's percentage of the total hours worked. That percentage was used to distribute the cash and charge card tips. I am concerned about why there is this murmuring to receive the tips at the close of shifts. I had thought about this situation a fair amount before deciding on the method of tip distribution that I had chosen. Are the employees thinking that I am not giving them all of their tips? Do they think that this system is unfair, as some shifts are much busier than others? Would they work harder to please customers if they were more directly impacted by the customers that they are dealing with? Our store layout is very open, and all customers can view what we are doing behind the dipping cabinets as well as at the cash register. It is a bad visual for an employee to be counting tip money and then trying to determine the amount each dipper receives, particularly if customers are waiting to be served. Most times, there is a fair amount of loose change in the tip bucket. How long will that take to count and distribute? Although it appears to be unfair that someone working on a slower shift will benefit from the hard work of a busier crew, that slower crew still needs to do all the same opening and closing tasks, including all restocking and clean-up. Do I want employees avoiding slower shifts? Conversely, by the method that I am using, will I create a reluctance to work during the busier times? Finally, because the tips are based on the percentage of hours worked, someone who helps make ice cream or comes into the clean receives those extra hours and a higher percentage of tips. I need employees to want to make ice cream.

I am trying to discuss this situation with employees. I have realized that I have not followed through on my promise to review performance after thirty days or ten shifts. I need to begin to do this. This would be a great time to try to understand the tip situation. One of the reasons that I have heard is that many times the young employees do not have enough money with them to maybe buy dinner or to make up the difference between their allotted large serving and the price of a sundae. I think I am going to write up an "I owe tip" coupon that a cash-short employee can exchange for a small amount of money from the tip bucket. I will still calculate tips for each employee as I have been doing, but pay an "I owe tip" employee that much less at the end of the week. I did not see this problem with the tips coming.

Often, you have to pick the battles that are worth fighting. How cash tips are determined is one of those battles that caused me to surrender. After speaking with most of my employees, I changed my policy and now have the tips divided as employees end their shift. They are asked to do the counting and dividing in the back, away from our customers, in an effort not to appear to be distracted from waiting on our customers. This new policy has taken a bit of work away from me and given it to our employees. This is not officially the way I thought Cherry Blossom Creamery would become more self-sufficient, but this revised policy in fact aligns with that goal.

Open five days in a row has made a serious dent in our ice cream supply. I decided to begin making ice cream on Memorial Day before we opened. I made ice cream again, most of Tuesday, concentrating on chocolates. For the past several weeks, Abby has been able to help me on Wednesdays. Not this week. I worked by myself, concentrating on the vanilla. Thursday, I did a few more flavors. Friday, I made strawberry ice cream with seasonal fresh strawberries. The cost of the strawberries is so steep that I can not make the fresh strawberry ice cream for the store. I did make enough to dip pints for all of my employees and for a few people who have been most generous in helping in our first ten weeks of operation. The ice cream is beyond delicious, and there is nothing added to enhance the strawberry flavor.

We have enough ice cream to open on Thursday, but can I sustain this level of making ice cream? The outside temperature has reached ninety-one, which still makes the temperature in the store even higher. It is now ninety-six. Working is extremely unpleasant. Our customers eating ice cream inside or out is far from ideal. The capacity of our air conditioning system has been totally overwhelmed by the higher temperatures and the amount of heat generated by the refrigeration equipment. We have to install mini-splits to supplement what we have. I gave the go-ahead. The money for this has to come from our personal checking, as Cherry Blossom Creamery is not generating positive cash flow as of yet. I had given a lot of thought to closing on Saturday because of the awful temperatures in the store, but fortunately, outside temperatures have moderated, and with the help of a couple of fans, we are open for the weekend.

We are beginning our twelfth week in operation. Even before opening the ice cream store, it has been my practice to break my goals into twelve-week segments. Twelve weeks is enough time to work on a project and often bring it to completion. It is also a time frame that allows for some evaluation of results. It is also a short enough time frame to impose deadlines or to abandon unproductive activities. Where are we at Cherry Blossom Creamery? On the one hand, I marvel at many of the tasks that we now routinely accomplish. Without my supervision, we are able to open, close, and serve our customers. Routine cleanliness has been maintained. The cash is always very close to the amount that the point of sale register indicates is appropriate. Less routine tasks, such as washing the lids and the dipping case collars, are more sporadically accomplished. Restocking the ice cream from the storage cabinet to the dipping cases shows signs of improvement. But how close are we to a self-sustaining operation? Quite a way away.

I have begun a list of what needs to be taught and monitored if we are to achieve that goal. This list is purposely operational in nature. It deals with what has to be accomplished if the store is to keep serving its customers, which does not include my direct involvement. The desire is great for me to just continue to do those tasks. They are not unpleasant, and I know, at least at this time, I can get them accomplished much more quickly than showing someone else how to do them. If I take that route, then this enterprise will never accomplish my stated goal of being self-sustaining. Since my staff is ever changing, I will have to train multiple employees on how to accomplish the less routine tasks. It is not yet a list that deals with vendor relationships, employee advancement or evaluation, or other larger picture concerns. It would be great to get to some of that more difficult list in a future twelve-week segment.

The one constant issue was, is, and looks like it will be forever is staff scheduling. This has to be on the current list of goals. I need to find a method that I am comfortable with and that the now fifteen young employees can buy into. Yes, I hired two more employees yesterday. I looked at Saturday's work schedule and saw that I had one employee to open and one employee to close. Abby and I checked with all the other eleven employees, and none of them could work. Desperation has resulted in two more paychecks to write. The extra work is frustrating, but I am also concerned that there will shortly come a time when everyone wants to work, and we will have too many employees to allow that to happen. I will be forced to choose my strongest employees if that occurs.

I never had a superstition about the number thirteen. In fact, I had chosen that post office box number for my mail-order sporting goods store. As that business is no more, maybe I should have been more mindful of the number thirteen. Superstition or not, our thirteenth week in business was very disappointing. It was our weakest revenue week since our first week. Combine that with the continued problems with our air conditioning, and I have a recipe for anxiety and second-guessing. Have we plateaued in our sales? Tourists do not seem to be finding us. When I have had employees available, I continue to overstaff, as I anticipate a much busier store. Second-guessing is now a full-time activity. Should I reduce staff? Do I even think about going forward with the popcorn station? Is my incompetence in engaging in proper social media what is holding our sales efforts back? Is this as big as this concept is going to be?

Whenever I am faced with this much noise, I find the only way to quiet that static is to make a list of short-term goals. I need to get much better signage in the store. I want to display our dairy-free single servings differently. This will require a new small display freezer. The doggie treats need an upgrade. I need to actually meet one-on-one with my employees and find out what they are happy about and what is not making them thrilled to be a Cherry Blossom Creamery employee. Continued exploration of new revenue sources, including popcorn, opera fudge, and even ice cream cakes, needs to continue. Finally, I need to find as many ways as possible to have my employees take on more tasks that I am currently responsible for. Self-sufficiency is still a long way off, but I must continue to strive for that, our most important goal.

Chapter 27

Cherry Blossom Creamery seems to have reached a plateau. Our sales are little changed from week to week. I had anticipated a gradual but sizable increase in customer traffic as we entered June and July. With that in mind, I staffed the shop accordingly. I need to examine that idea. Our percentage of employee cost to overall revenue is way out of line. I need to reduce the number of employees per shift. I think that this is something that our employees want to happen as well. I acquiesced to the employee's request that the tips be distributed at the end of each shift. They are taking care of this task themselves and making sure that the counting is done away from our customers' eyes. The employees understand that the fewer people on a shift will result in higher cash tips for the smaller number of staff working.

A new idea has emerged that I am seriously considering. If we are to lessen the number of employees per shift, why not open more days as well? This is an experiment that I find intriguing. This should increase our sales and still allow for our employees to work the same or more shifts than they had done with our overstaffed schedule.

Another idea that I am investigating is the purchase of a gourmet popcorn station. I visited with one of my suppliers while they demonstrated how to make popcorn. The setup is about eight feet in length, made to evoke the memory of a popcorn wagon. The front is plexiglass, which allows separation from our customers. There is a popping area. There are two kettles that allow us to make two different kinds of popcorn at a time. There are two separate areas to cool for each of the flavors. The popcorn can be bagged and sold immediately or shelved for future sales.

There is a lot to untangle with this idea. There is a considerable expense involved in purchasing the popcorn station. On one hand, I feel the need to reduce the total hours that my employees are working, while possibly requiring more hours to man the popcorn station. Many other questions arise. How will customers other than our existing ones learn that we sell gourmet popcorn? There are quite a few additional supplies that I will need to purchase. How will I find storage space for these ingredients when storage space is already in short supply? Once the popcorn is made, how do we display the finished product? We will need proper labels. Is this the best use of my time and money? Am I trying to do too much too soon?

It has been two weeks since I attended the popcorn demonstration, and I still cannot decide what is the best decision for Cherry Blossom Creamery. I am certain that I do not have the same faith in my concept as I had when I opened the store. If I thought that our ice cream sales would grow significantly, then it would make perfect sense to purchase the popcorn station and add it to our thriving store. I am just not sure if this ice cream idea is going to prosper and grow. Without a significant customer base, the idea of making popcorn as part of a show for our customers who are in the store appears a bit lame. If there are only a couple of customers sitting there, then making popcorn will fizzle. I spoke with my sales representative, and he told me that I need not hurry this decision. I can only feel my whole body giving a sigh of relief with this time extension.

Chapter 28

I often hear some of my friends say that they are participating in golf or tennis, or pickleball because it passes the time. Maybe they perceive their days as being long, and those days are part of a calendar that moves slowly. That is not my worry. I am guessing it is not a worry for most people operating their own business.

It seems operating your own business causes one to perceive the calendar differently. Much of the time, your mind is living in a date that does not correspond with the actual date. There is constant planning for the future. That future may be tomorrow, but usually it is several weeks or months ahead. I often think that I am living in those future months that my mind is planning. It is actually July, but I am inhabiting September. Every day passes too quickly, and seasons disappear while I am working on what Cherry Blossom Creamery needs to become. I notice the crepe myrtle is in full blossom in my backyard, and I ask myself if I even noticed the day lilies blooming in June. I am living in September while barely noticing August, which is the month that is actually here, and realizing that I have pretty much missed the months of June and July.

If I am to create what I have in my mind for Cherry Blossom Creamery, there will always be unresolved problems and opportunities. It is my hope that as we solve the current problems that the new opportunities will be just as interesting as the ones we are currently pursuing.

While we had the summer employees, I decided to make a commitment to being open every day beginning in late July and ending in mid-August. I wanted to test whether or not customers would find us on Monday, Tuesday and Wednesday, which were days that we were not normally open. I also needed to test if we could maintain an adequate supply of ice cream. Two weeks into this test, and we have had excellent customer response. With the help of several of our employees, I have been able to produce enough ice cream to keep the cases fully stocked. I have decided to extend our everyday of being open for at least another week and maybe even longer. It will all depend on employee availability.

We are entering our twenty-fifth day in succession that Cherry Blossom Creamery has been open. We are going to continue to be open every day for at least another week. Our customers have been very receptive to our expanded hours. Scheduling the staff continues to be challenging, and only going to get more so as school begins in another week. The extracurricular activities, field hockey, tennis, lacrosse, and so many more have already begun. Looking at the kids' schedules, it is evident that I will once again have to change our store hours. None of my employees can get there by two o'clock. I need to change hours to four to nine, knowing that in a month or so, I will be changing to four to eight as darkness returns much earlier in the day. This is confusing to our customers, but I have no employees who can work that early in the day.

Staffing the dipping and serving of our ice cream is just one of the issues that I must resolve over the next months. The vision I had of this being an ice cream store, but also a purveyor of curated and gourmet snacks, has not materialized. I am barely able to make enough ice cream to keep up with the demand. The occasional Pappy cracker sold just reminds me of how little of my vision has been brought forth. I need to hire people to help to and eventually to make our ice cream to supplement my efforts.

They also need to be able to help with whatever snacks or ice cream, cakes or other ideas I have. I don't know where to begin to find those employees. They need to be enthusiastic about our products. They need to be available in the mornings. I am fearful that Cherry Blossom Creamery is taking over my life. I cannot let this occur. If I cannot hire needed employees, then I need to scale back this effort and make this more of a hobby and less of a business.

The cracks are beginning to show. We have been open for thirty-two days in a row, and that stress test has produced some visible cracks in our procedures. I can not make enough ice cream to keep up with our sales. This problem will only get worse as my employees return to high school or college. My help in making ice cream is fast disappearing. I have had the great good fortune of finding an old friend who is going to help me make ice cream. At least I hope. Other issues have arisen. There are errors in my ordering of basic supplies. We need jacketed cones, and instead, we have ones without the jackets. This requires us to wrap all the cones in a napkin when we are serving. This creates more trash as well as more expense with the extra napkins. Opening and closing procedures have become more erratic. Our employees are busier than ever with customers, and their attention to detail, such as unplugging the hot fudge machine or properly sanitizing the milkshake machine, has suffered. There is difficulty in finding where needed supplies, whether they be cones, dishes, waffle chips, or garbage bags, can be found. This is mostly my problem. I need to organize everything better, but by the time I have ice cream made, schedules generated, and deposits made and bills paid, I lack the energy to do anything else.

Chapter 29

My vision for Cherry Blossom Creamery has become unclear. I must commit to paper what I now see my store becoming. I must be a visionary, or I will be left with a very nice ice cream store, but one that has not reached the potential that I had in mind when creating this enterprise. Six months of ordering supplies, making dairy-free and regular ice cream, occasionally producing dog treats and pappy crackers, and tackling the ever elusive employee scheduling has forced me to view Cherry Blossom Creamery more as a job and less as a creative enterprise.

Now is the time to find the requisite energy and inspiration to map out how this store is to become what I had envisioned. Six months of operation have tested many of the concepts upon which I opened the store. I need to use that experience and modify some of the ideas that I had when we first opened. I also need to push beyond what we are now doing and create new products, systems, and relationships. In less than two weeks, Sue and I will be heading west to visit several National Parks. If I am unable to find the time to clarify my vision before we leave, then I will attempt to do so while we are on vacation.

A troubling trend has become apparent this past week. It is the week before Labor Day, and our revenue has dropped considerably. It was my hope to remain open until the end of the year. But if this drop in revenue continues or becomes even more drastic, I will need to reevaluate that idea. This trend is calling into question our hours of operation and our level of employee staffing. Not the best frame of mind to outline my vision of Cherry Blossom Creamery.

Sue and I spent two glorious weeks in the west visiting Rocky Mountain Park, Arches, Capital Reef, Bryce, and Zion. The scenery was breathtaking. The weather was gorgeous. We stopped in at least six ice cream stores. Popcorn was in almost every place we stopped. The decision to add popcorn, I believe, has been made. On a very positive note, Cherry Blossom Creamery was open every day we were gone. Our employees did a great job. The store looked great when we returned. They handled all the challenges that came their way. Our supply of ice cream had dwindled significantly. It was time to gear up the production.

Once we were back, another problem had been successfully disposed of. Except for a few glitches, we now have a flavor screen and a menu screen. It is a great improvement, making our store look much more professional. There are still signage challenges that I hope to address soon, but a project that began in the middle of the summer is now done as we go into mid-October. This is a lesson in patience that I need to remember as I contemplate all that is left to be done. I hope that this will allow for continued training and for each of our employees to feel more empowered and confident in their work.

There was one more task to complete before we could close out the year. Our flavor screen, although very professional in appearance, has been a nightmare for all of our employees to initiate the changes that need to happen in order to keep it accurate. I decided to repurpose the flavor screen to highlight some of the services and products we offer. Instead of a flavor screen, I asked Ed, my daughter's father-in-law law to build a retro-looking board complete with hooks and flavor choices. All that any of us needed to do to change our flavors was remove the flavor from the board and hang the new one in its place. This is going to be a big improvement.

Chapter 30

When I set out to record my journey as an ice cream entrepreneur, I was confident that a story of how a small business is created would be of some general interest. I was fairly confident that at the end of the story, a successful business would have been formed. As I enter the first winter of Cherry Blossom Creamery's existence, I am less certain of that successful outcome.

The more mature Cherry Blossom Creamery that I have imagined is far from what we have so far created. Fresh handmade ice cream is always the base upon which everything else is built, but there needs to be so much more. At a minimum, we need the store to be merchandised with many other handmade snacks such as popcorn, chocolate-coated candies, and meadow teas. We also need snack combinations that we create, as well as quality chips, etc.

The store needs shelving and décor. It needs to retain its clean lines while offering so much more to our customers. Our customer base at this time is not large enough to support this idea. Conversely, if I do not offer this enhanced experience, I do not think we will grow our revenue and customer support to allow Cherry Blossom Creamery to become the jewel I want it to be.

Aside from the sales concerns, the lack of adequate employees is creating quite a worry. If we are to introduce the new items that I feel are necessary to our continued growth, I will need to either find more or a different kind of employee. At a minimum, I will need to have my current employees commit to more hours. Can we build systems that will allow us to make the items we will need? If we successfully create these items, will there be enough customers to purchase them? Do I have the drive to get where this company needs to go, or do I settle for a fairly comfortable, if very busy, life that includes great ice cream and a very cute store?

As the year is coming to an end, I must evaluate our financial position. It is not great. Our employee costs, as expressed in a percentage of sales, are way too high. Our material to make our great ice cream is too expensive. Our overhead is more than I had anticipated. If our revenue remains the same for next year, I believe we will be able to reduce employee costs as we do not need to have the level of staffing we had when everything was new. The ingredient costs will improve as I continue to find new vendors that offer better prices or, more importantly, less shipping costs. Our overhead is not something I can easily modify. The answer to all of these concerns is that we must increase our sales revenue. Will the revenue grow just because we have built a customer base from this first year? Will the addition of gourmet popcorn make a huge difference? Can we produce enough great snacks to matter? This is a pivot moment. Either we significantly increase our top line, or I reduce the size of my vision for Cherry Blossom Creamery.

The popcorn machine has arrived. I had modifications made to the setup to better accommodate the vast majority of our staff who, like me, are not very tall. We also painted the front to match our colors, replacing the strident yellow that presented itself to us. A morning of training, and we are off to the popcorn races. It is surprisingly simple to operate, and the popcorn is really good. We still have to iron out some challenges as to packaging, but we will get there. One week in and our revenue for the first popcorn week was thirty-eight percent better than it had been for any of the past three weeks. Will this upsurge signal the much-needed top-line increase Cherry Blossom Creamery was searching for? If nothing else, the shelves that we purchased that are now filled with beautiful popcorn have made the upstairs a much more interesting place. Integrating our other snacks into the popcorn area is my next project.

We did learn one thing, though, about this time of year. Being open on the evening of Super Bowl Sunday is ill-advised. Note to self, next year close at five o'clock.

February and March pass with little drama. Our hours of operation are now five days a week and begin at 4:00 and end at 8:00. Staffing is rarely a problem with these limited hours. The need to replenish our ice cream is so reduced that I am only making ice cream once a week. As awful as the weather is some days, we have always had someone come into the store and purchase ice cream. March has been quite mild, and with that decent weather, our revenue has been surprisingly decent. I am looking forward to a strong April and the second season.

Chapter 31

The holiday season is full of parties. Sue and I got to attend the annual Hershey Art Association Christmas party. It is probably my favorite party, although truth be told, we don't really go to that many parties. For this party, everyone brings a great food dish. There are only about fifty people, several of whom I enjoy seeing. There is always entertainment. This year, it was the Hershey High School Jazz band. They were terrific. Great food, decent company, lively entertainment and a party that lasts about two hours. What could be better? Not to mention, we brought a lot of our small containers of ice cream, and I received great compliments. At the same time, they were not paying for this ice cream, so the compliments really flowed.

Behind the stage where the jazz band played was a very interesting mural that was composed of ads for businesses that were once a part of our area. There was a general store, a bakery, a dairy, a plumber, and several more. They all shared two things. The businesses all looked like places I would like to shop, and all of them were no longer in business. It made me reflect. Aside from a very few businesses, such as Hershey or Coca-Cola, or Gilette, businesses come and go. Almost always, they are opened with great enthusiasm. Eventually, there is either no longer a need for that business or, more likely, there is no mechanism to allow it to continue after the death or retirement of the founder.

I fully realize that should I no longer be able to operate Cherry Blossom Creamery, there is no plan in place or even the effort to make a plan for the store to continue. That fact is alarming. If I am blessed with a few years to develop our store, I will make it a goal to try to determine a possible path for its continued existence. Another realization came upon me. I certainly know that change is inevitable. That change means that most likely, Cherry Blossom Creamery has a few years to shine brightly and then probably stop shining altogether. It is my goal to use that window of time to create the best ice cream and snack store our town has seen. If fifty years from now, an ad for Cherry Blossom Creamery is hanging behind a jazz band performing at a great holiday party, I hope that those people attending that party would have wished they could have visited our store.

We are entering the final week of the year. A few more days and Cherry Blossom Creamery will close for about five weeks. It has been open for nine months, and although there is much left to be done, I am optimistic about next season. I have taken the school vacation time as an opportunity to meet with as much of my staff as can be scheduled. I have named our get-togethers as training sessions, which we need, but more importantly, I am trying to remind everyone of our core values. That we are attentive, present, friendly, competent and willing to say yes to what our customers want. At the same time, we do need to get better at a few items. The most worrisome for me is portion control. To that end, I have set up a dipping contest for each of the get-togethers. Each employee dips a child-size cup, a regular-size cup, and a large-size cone. These are each weighed, and the result is recorded and compared to the weight we desire. After the three dips, the employee is allowed to redo the worst one. The employee with the least variation from the ideal is given a twenty-dollar bill. It was fun to see the competitive nature of some of the kids. What all of us saw was that as a group, we need to work on this. Having consistent and correct serving sizes is key to customer satisfaction and to our profitability. This training is something that 1 need to incorporate into daily opening times until we get where we need to go.

I have developed a checklist of the many competencies that our employees need to master. Such things as operating the soft serve machine, making popcorn, changing the flavor board, and so many. At the end of the training session, I had each employee check the items they were more comfortable with.

Chapter 32

Year 2

Once we closed on December 29, I began immediately to work on year two. There were a few items that I know we needed to address. First, we needed to do a thorough cleaning and perform routine maintenance of all of our equipment. Commercial Refrigeration was scheduled to do the maintenance in January. Before their arrival, we were able to move all of the equipment and do a thorough cleaning.

It had been apparent that many of our less mobile customers were challenged by our walkway and two steps leading to the stairs in the front of our building. For ease of access, we installed a handrail along the sidewalk and steps. This did not in any way provide handicap access, but it was a marked improvement.

Knowing that we would be making more flavors of popcorn as well as other snacks, it was important to allow sampling. I purchased a small table that would allow us to provide those samples.

Finally, I had to make some tough decisions. Do we keep the soft serve machine? Do we keep the soda dispensing machine? I am keeping the soft serve machine for another season. Matt assures me that he will clean the machine weekly as needed. I am searching for better flavors so that we can more fully utilize this very expensive and little-used piece of equipment. We have utilized it to make ice cream sandwiches, which have sold very well. I don't know if this is justification enough to keep it in our store, but I seem unable to make the decision to remove the machine.

When it came to the question of whether or not to retain the soda fountain machine, I felt that the best way to decide about the fountain sodas was to send a text to all of our employees and ask them if this is something they really would like to keep. One of the few perks that the employees enjoyed was unlimited free soda when they were working. The response was that as long as we had water available, they were fine with losing their benefit of sodas while they worked. I can understand their dentist's concern for loss of revenue with fewer cavities during our employee's next check-up.

Sue and my Florida holiday has taken place while we are closed. It was our first trip to St. Augustine, where we spent two weeks with old friends playing tennis, walking, and eating at great restaurants. Of course, we visited all the ice cream stores that were in the area.

Opening day is February 3, one day after Groundhog Day. This is National Ice Cream for Breakfast Day- a little-known and poorly observed holiday- that is, until now. Through email and Facebook, we promoted a cold-weather ice cream breakfast. Serving waffles and ice cream as well as pop tarts and ice cream, we had at least sixty customers arrive before noon. It was a great feeling to have customers waiting out the door. We had only been closed for five weeks, but many of those who ventured out in the cold were very happy to be eating our wow ice cream once again.

It is February, the middle of winter, but customers still do show up. From the amount of revenue we generate, in all likelihood, we would be better off closed. I try to look at this from a different perspective. It costs something to acquire any customer. Either you offer a promotion that lowers your profit margin, or you buy some type of advertising, which still costs money. Our being open allows new customers to find and hopefully love our store. Yes, employees need to be paid, and the utilities keep sending bills, but I like this method of finding new customers. It has an organic feel to growing our store.

Chapter 33

Late April 2024

I am wrestling with the most doubt that I have had since opening. I am uncertain about the viability of Cherry Blossom Creamery. We opened in April of last year. I finally had sales numbers to compare to as we enter our second season. Those numbers are shocking. I cannot make sense of what is occurring. We are so far behind the numbers we did last year that all I can do is worry about why. Is our ice cream not as good as I thought it was? Is our staff not treating our customers with the attention and friendliness that I thought they were? People found our store last season. How is it that our location this season is not as popular as it was last year?

This last month has been a very emotionally difficult time for me. I have concerns about the continuation of Cherry Blossom Creamery when it is posting such dismal sales numbers. I have also learned that my oldest and closest friend has stage four cancer. I am depressed. I drag myself through the tasks that must be done at the store. Upon their completion, I am unable to muster the energy to add new snacks or think about better promotions. At this moment, much of this adventure feels pointless. At the same time, the prospect of doing nothing all day feels like surrendering to my inevitable mortality. There are many reasons to question starting a new enterprise so late in life, but maybe the most impactful is the number of friends and acquaintances who are struggling with life-altering medical issues. My concern for their well-being is genuine, and their issues are a reminder to me as to how small the creation of Cherry Blossom Creamery truly is. Our sales are off by 41% for April. This is hardly what I had anticipated for our second year.

The calendar has flipped to May, and we are now open seven days a week. I am not sure that adding more payroll costs to flat sales is a remedy for success, but I must do something. Slowly, sales begin to match last May. Our staff is much more confident and competent, which allows me to do a leaner schedule. Our percent of employee costs to revenue is much lower. May ends, and we have matched last year's sales for the month. Our employee costs were down by 19%. Maybe we are headed in the right direction.

The weather has turned midsummer hot and humid, and it is only June. It is ice cream weather, and our customers seem to agree. We have had our two best weeks ever sandwiched around two other solid weeks. Now my concern is, can we make enough ice cream? Can I keep the store staffed?

The store follows a comfortable routine. Monday, I inventory our stock of ice cream that is sitting in our storage freezer. My order of basic supplies, such as cones, ice cream cups, toppings, etc., is also delivered and gets put away. Tuesday, the new ice cream mix and soft serve gallons are delivered and stored in our refrigerator. Wednesday and Thursday, Margo or Abby, and I make ice cream. Thursday, I place the order to Dehart for next week. Throughout the week, the employees are making brownies, or enrobing cones, or crushing Oreos, or crumbling Graham crackers, or making ice cream sandwiches, or cutting up fruit for the topping bar or for our ice cream production. I even sneak in the opportunity to make some dairy-free or sugar-free ice cream on days that we are not making regular ice cream. The sense of routine is so strong that the weeks fly by. It seems like only yesterday I was sighing in relief that our sales numbers for May were as good as last year, when July and August continue to surpass previous sales.

Where has the summer gone? I believe we have an exceptional ice cream store, but can it become self-sustaining? I am concerned that too much of what I do, I have not been able to, through better training, pass on to any of my employees. As much as this is troubling, the question that overwhelms me in mid-August is: where have my employees gone?

Chapter 34

Keeping the doors open

From May 1 of our second year cherry blossom creamery has been open every day. It is now the end of August, and I am certain that the decision to be open every day has added much clarity for our customers and has allowed us to post steady, decent to good revenue results every day. We have adjusted to this reality rather well. We are able to make enough ice cream even with the increase in demand. Part of the reason for this is that I have trained two to three other people who are comfortable making our ice cream. There are meticulous recipes for each flavor. We use the same ingredients every time we make the same flavor. It is only because these folks truly care that the ice cream is made correctly and consistently that has allowed me to have a bit of a break from the manufacturing of the ice cream. Our popcorn and our dog treats, and our snacks are kept in stock and are made by our employees. What I have not resolved is having employees to cover all of our hours that we are open.

My answer to shifts that are not covered has been hiring new employees. We have lost several good employees to college. We have compromised availability for many of the kids as they are in soccer, cross country, field hockey, cheerleading, lacrosse, golf, and band. They have extracurricular activities almost every night and sometimes on weekends. There have been instances where I reviewed the upcoming work schedule, and I was certain that we would have to close due to no employee coverage. Realizing how badly this would impact customer relations, I have been able to find new hires who could plug the holes in our work schedule. That action is not without consequences. Although our training was never exhaustive, at least there was some effort made to work with new hires when they would not feel the need to initially interact much with customers, but instead learn what they needed to master to do this job.. With the desperation that is inherent in hiring immediately, we are throwing our new people right into the mix, hoping that they will catch on to whatever they are being asked to do. This haphazard training approach begs for much inconsistency in our portion controls.

Alongside the shortcomings in how we handle customers, there is a second portion of what our employees are asked to do. There is a learning curve that allows our more experienced employees to be able to do many things other than serve customers. They know how to restock ice cream from the storage freezer to the dipping cases and to the display freezers. They know how to chocolate dip waffle cones. They know how to make ingredient labels. They know how to make popcorn or doggie treats, or pappy crackers. As more and more of the hours that we are open are taken by fresh hires, the difficulty in getting the tasks that need to be done only increases. There are twenty-six people on our staff. This is far too many. It is a problem that I need to ponder and eventually address.

When I decided to take this journey, I promised myself that this business would not take over my life. I have not been altogether successful in that goal. I truly expect and enjoy spending several hours each day with Cherry Blossom Creamery. With the difficulty in keeping the hours covered, I have felt anxiety whenever I make plans to be away, either in distance or time from the store. Even if I may not be actually at the store, I am not making plans or participating in activities that take me very far from it. I am fully aware that more documentation on how all of the tasks required to operate Cherry Blossom Creamery are needed. Even with that documentation, a better training program needs to be begun. I have begun to ask my more experienced employees to do that documentation. I want them to think that they had never worked in an ice cream store before, and this is their first day. Please write down everything that would be helpful to that employee. Gathering this information now, as we close year two, will hopefully allow us to enter year three better equipped to be competent, consistent, and more self-sustaining.

Chapter 35

INFLECTION POINT

Writing this book, I have had to follow the timeline in the formation and development of Cherry Blossom Creamery. I could continue to follow the maturation of my store and write about year three and then year four. It would be interesting to me, but I am unsure if this narrative would be engaging for you, the reader. I have decided that it is time to end this book as we end year two.

It is a great feeling to realize that there is still so much to do. There is no ultimate vision for Cherry Blossom Creamery. Instead, I hope that we can improve on what we do one small step at a time. We need our customers not just to leave with a smile, but the determination that they will return to what we hope is a one-of-a-kind experience.

Cherry Blossom Creamery is at an inflection point. Year two saw a decent increase in revenue, more controlled employee costs, and a very modest profit. That profit occurred because I, as the owner, did not take any pay for the year's work. Our store, like most small businesses, suffers from a deficiency in our top line—our gross revenue. A business can reduce employee costs, overhead, and even the cost of materials needed to produce whatever the business is selling. This effort will allow the business to possibly be more profitable or at least extend its life expectancy, but it is only an act of triage. A business only succeeds if the top line or revenue is able to attain the proper number. At this time, I believe that the sales revenue number necessary for Cherry Blossom Creamer is around two hundred thousand dollars per year. For year three to reach that goal, we need a very healthy increase in sales. In order to do that, we need to make Cherry Blossom Creamery a destination for folks who visit or live in Central Pennsylvania.

So many questions, challenges, and opportunities. Can the store become profitable enough for someone else to purchase it? Can a new owner bring the energy to open satellite locations? Would that owner be interested in attending soccer tournaments and selling ice cream? Will the freeze-dried ice cream become a major revenue source? Can Cherry Blossom Creamery effectively market to local restaurants and grocery stores?

The most likely ending to this story will be that this effort, this adventure, will end when I no longer wish to or become unable to operate Cherry Blossom Creamery. Sad as that outcome would be, I believe that we were able to create a business that produced an excellent and unique product, merchandised in an attractive setting, and served by an attentive, friendly, and competent staff of teenagers. I think this is a story worth telling.

www.ingramcontent.com/pod-product-compliance
Lightning Source LLC
LaVergne TN
LVHW022216200926
848481LV00006B/1991
* 9 7 9 8 9 0 0 0 1 8 0 4 1 *